The 21 DAY FINANCIAL FAST

The 21 DAY FINANCIAL FAST

Your Path to
FINANCIAL PEACE AND FREEDOM

Previously published as
The Power to Prosper: 21 Days to Financial Freedom

MICHELLE SINGLETARY

ZONDERVAN

The 21-Day Financial Fast
Copyright © 2010, 2014 by Michelle Singletary
Previously published under the title *The Power to Prosper*

This title is also available as a Zondervan ebook.
Visit www.zondervan.com/ebooks.

Requests for information should be addressed to:

Zondervan, 3900 *Sparks Dr. SE, Grand Rapids, Michigan* 49546

This edition: 978-0-310-33833-8

Library of Congress Cataloging-in-Publication Data
    The power to prosper : 21 days to financial freedom / Michelle Singletary.
        p.   cm.
    Includes bibliographical references.
    ISBN 978-0-310-32038-8 (softcover)
    1. Finance, Personal — Religious aspects — Christianity. 2. Finance, Personal — Biblical
teaching. I. Title.
HG179.S5144 2009
332.024 — dc22   2009028364

The 21-Day Financial Fast is a practical guide on personal finance. There are no guarantees offered in the 21-day financial fast program. Individual results will vary. Readers are cautioned to undertake the recommendations and assignments with caution, using their own judgment or after seeking professional advice from legal or financial professionals about their individual circum-stances. Additionally, certain information such as website addresses may change.

Interior design and composition: Greg Johnson/Textbook Perfect
Cover design: Studio Gearbox
Cover photography: Sade Dennis

Printed in the United States of America

24 25 26 27 28 LBC 64 63 62 61 60

I dedicate this book to my children,
Monique Olivia, Kevin, and Jillian.
You've endured countless lessons
and long lectures about money,
sometimes with rolled eyes,
but mostly with good humor.

I pray that you always have
God's peace in your finances
and in every part of your lives.

I also dedicate this book to
Juanita Ann Waller,
a friend whom I dearly miss.
Juanita's faith helped her find
financial peace and became debt-free,
and as a result, her journey became
an inspiration for so many.

Contents

Acknowledgments..11

Prosperity on Purpose.......................................14

Part One

Why a Financial Fast?

Day 1   Twenty-One Days to Financial Freedom 25

Day 2   A Promise of Prosperity 39

Day 3   God's Generosity 48

Day 4   Tithing Today......................................58

Part Two

Fasting for a Better Financial Life

Day 5   The Evils of Entitlement 73

Day 6   You Can't Buy Contentment.........................82

Day 7   The Benefits of Budgeting 88

Day 8   The Salvation of Saving...........................107

Day 9   Diversification Delivers..........................119

Day 10 Marrying Your Money 127

Day 11 Leave a Legacy of Good Money Sense 134

Part Three

Fasting to Avoid Financial Drama

Day 12   The Devil Is in the Debt 149

Day 13   The Curse of Credit. 166

Day 14   Cosigning Is Crazy. 177

Day 15   Guard Against Greed 186

Day 16   The Caregiver Cliff 194

Part Four

Fasting for Financial Peace

Day 17   Perpetual Peace. 207

Day 18   Broken Bonds 213

Day 19   Strengthen Stewardship 218

Day 20   Relationships Rescued. 224

Day 21   Financial Freedom 227

Appendixes

1. Blank Budget Worksheet. 235

2. What's Next: Starting Your 30-Day Spending Journal 241

3. How to Start a 21-Day Fast in Your Church 243

4. Sample Daily Fast Journal Page 244

5. Financial Fast Scripture Verses 246

Index 249

Acknowledgments

I can't begin this book without first giving thanks to God. I know now that even during the times I was down and feeling alone, He was right there carrying me. It was God who allowed me to be placed in the care of my grandmother, Big Mama. And it was my grandmother who taught me to think about money in a way that would someday be a blessing to members of my family, my church, my community, and millions of newspaper readers, radio listeners, and television viewers across the country.

I also thank God for leading me to First Baptist Church of Glenarden. Under the leadership of Pastor John K. Jenkins Sr. and his wife, First Lady Trina Jenkins, I have grown tremendously in my faith. It was at First Baptist, and with the encouragement of my pastor and his wife, that I began conducting the 21-day financial fast.

I will forever be grateful and thankful for the members of Prosperity Partners Ministry and for its incredible leadership team. It has been a privilege to serve with the following individuals: Adrienne Alexander, Olivia Baker, Alton Croslin, Deenice Galloway, Min. Angelia Rowe Garner, Trinita McCall, Tonya Muse, Yolanda Oliver, Michael Rhim, Kiesha Samee'Ud-Deen, the late Juanita Ann Waller, and Bethany Williams. This dedicated group work hard and diligently to support a ministry that has helped so many to get their financial lives in order. I also want to thank the staff at First Baptist Church of Glenarden (especially the audio visual team) and the many members of my church who together continue to show me unwavering support. In particular,

I'm grateful for Barbara and Malcolm Streeter, two friends who always have my back.

This book would not have been possible without my wonderful and hardworking agent, Richard Abate. The staff at Zondervan, including Bob Hudson, Karen Campbell, Courtney Lasater, Becky Philpott, and Marcy Schorsch, has been fantastic. I couldn't have had a better and more thoughtful editor than Sandy Vander Zicht. The entire Zondervan team who worked on this book has just been wonderful. This has truly been a team effort.

I am very blessed to work at the *Washington Post* and with an incredible group of people who have been tremendously supportive of my book endeavors. I'm especially appreciative of my former research assistant, Charity Brown, my current assistant, Tia Lewis, and my past and present editors, Steve Levingston, Gregory Schneider, Kelly Johnson, and James Hill, and Alan Shearer of the *Washington Post* Writers Group.

Writing a book often comes with much sacrifice. The friends and family of the author are the ones who make the process easier. So it is with much love that I thank my friends and family, especially Terri and Larry Ames, Debbie and Pat Berry, Alexa Steele, Sade Dennis, and Wiley Hall. I couldn't have made it through the long nights and lack of sleep without your encouragement. You made me laugh sometimes when all I wanted to do was cry. Thanks to Robin Tarver and Nicole Rochester for letting me vent. One of my biggest fans is my brother, Michael Singletary. I am so blessed to have a brother who is so incredibly enthusiastic about my work. Just as supportive is my extended family, including my mother, sister-in-law, Kim, in-laws, aunts, uncles, nieces, nephews, and cousins.

Also I wouldn't have had the time to work on the book without the help of my dear sister, Monique Reynolds, and my loving godmother, Lois Thompson, and godsister, Courtney Bethea, who all helped with my children.

I owe so much to my children, Olivia, Kevin, and Jillian, who checked on me and gave me many hugs to encourage me during this project. They even sacrificed several family movie nights so I could work on the book.

Finally, there's my husband, Kevin. I have no doubt that God sent me this wonderful, loving, patient man who pushes me to be a better Christian, wife, mother, and friend. Even more, I'm blessed that he has joined me in directing Prosperity Partners. It has been a joy to work alongside a man who has such great love for the Lord and his family.

Prosperity on Purpose

If you want to be rich, change. Grow. Get organized. Make the decision that you want to prosper.

Those are the lesson I've learned since I first created the 21-day financial fast in 2005. At the time, I was fasting from food when it occurred to me that the same concept of discipline and self-denial might be applied to people's finances. My epiphany for the fast came long before the Great Recession. In fact, the country was enjoying growth and prosperity when I had the idea for the fast. Yet I was concerned and weary from watching people struggle with their finances even though times were good.

In the years to come, the economy will both prosper and decline. The employment numbers will rise and fall. And, as we learned in the last recession, home values can drop as well as increase. The stock market will do what it has always done — we will have bearish (bad) and bullish (good) years. But through it all, you need to be steady with how you handle your money. What never changes is the work it takes to create lasting wealth. Real net worth is created by hard work, delayed gratification, and financial education.

So I'm asking you to work at your wealth building. I'm challenging you to take twenty-one days and curb your consumerism. Buy only what's necessary. For three weeks, stop using credit. Use the twenty-one days to consider what being rich means to you.

And in case you're wondering, when I use the word *rich*, I'm not talking about material wealth. I'm talking about the peace that comes when you've done all you can to wisely use the financial resources God has entrusted to you. The 21-day financial fast is about preparing yourself to prosper and leaving a legacy for your family that allows them to prosper, too.

The fast is also about getting your financial house in order. Aren't you tired of the chaos and clutter? When you get your financial house in order, it directly impacts your financial life.

Let me explain.

I've dealt with a lot of death. My grandfather, brother, and father-in-law died from lung cancer. They died with their affairs not in order. I contrast their situations to what happened when a close friend, Juanita Ann Waller, whose testimonies you'll read in this book, died in an automobile accident in 2012. She was the most ardent supporter of my 21-day financial fast. She took it to a level even I haven't achieved.

Juanita left her personal financial affairs and her apartment in an astonishingly organized condition. She got her finances and house in order, never anticipating she would die at age fifty-four. She left a will, life insurance, and the necessary paperwork to take care of her estate. But there was a higher level of organization in her affairs than I've ever seen. She not only freed herself from debt, she freed herself from wanting, buying, and accumulating too much stuff.

Juanita had a place for everything. She catalogued what was in her file cabinet. She had a notebook that detailed what was in each cabinet drawer. As a result, when several of us who were her friends went to pack up her belongings, we didn't have to look through her private papers to be able to label the boxes. She kept binders of her awards and accolades, including a letter to her signed by President Obama, protected behind sheets of plastic. She had sent Obama an email saying she was praying for him, and the White House responded.

There wasn't a single junk drawer in her apartment. There were no stacks of papers on her desk threatening to unleash an avalanche of craziness on the floor. Nor did she have bags of papers stuffed in corners or in her closets. She didn't even have a trash can because there wasn't much waste to throw away. Her closets weren't over-stuffed. Her pantry and refrigerator weren't overstocked with food that would take months to eat or go to waste. There wasn't a single item in any room that we could tell went unused for very long.

My friend was a financial fast devotee striving to get people to reduce their consumption and material possessions. Her place was so tidy and uncluttered that I wept. It made me ashamed of my personal living space, my disorderly office, and my hoarding of things that long ago should have been tossed, recycled, or donated.

Over the years, I've promised myself to get organized. But when-ever I clean my office, it's cluttered again a few weeks later with piles of papers sitting in stacks on the floor.

Just think about this: If you were to die, how long would it take for people to go through your stuff? How many hours would they have to take off from their jobs to find and organize your personal property? Could they find your will? Where would they look for any instructions on your estate? Have you written down in a secure place the passwords to your computer or phone so friends and family can contact people if you pass away?

Juanita wasn't obsessive with her orderliness. She was organized for a purpose. As we were packing her possessions, we all felt embar-rassed — but for ourselves, not Juanita. We, in our abundance, saw a woman who kept only what she needed, knowing it was more than enough. That's what Juanita learned from the fast.

We all pledged to spend some time organizing and getting rid of stuff as a remembrance of Juanita, who gave an abundance of hugs, in addition to her time helping others achieve financial peace. We promised her that we'd get our houses in order.

I want you to get what Juanita got. I want you to understand that you have so much already. I want you to take your prosperity seri-ously by consuming less, shunning debt, and organizing your finan-cial life. I want you to be rich in the way Juanita was rich.

THIS FAST IS FOR YOU

The Bible is the key source for this book. Even if you are not religious, the Old and New Testaments give the best and most basic advice on how to handle your money — in good times and bad. We've seen what the world can evolve into by listening to and following the corrupt and greedy advice of financial companies and advisers. The Bible says, "The wisdom of this world is foolishness in God's sight" (1 Cor. 3:19). So why not give Scripture a chance to change your financial life?

I love the way the Bible provides a roadmap to wealth — it promises prosperity, but prosperity with a purpose as a means to an end that isn't about stuff. It all boils down to this: The more you get, the more you are commanded to give. This universal concept is one we all can and should embrace.

The key feature of this book is the financial fast. But if you think you can do this 21-day financial fast on your own, you are mistaken. It's going to take discipline. The discipline of fasting forces you to turn your focus away from the things of the world — credit and shopping — and reach out to God. Fasting at its essence is about self-denial. And Lord knows there's a need these days for people to deny their desires. For it's these wanton desires that have caused financial pain for so many.

Fasting is also about obedience. Scripture gives us many examples of people who fasted. Moses fasted. Elijah fasted. David fasted. Daniel fasted. And Jesus fasted.

This fast is for you if you're at your financial wit's end. This fast is for you if the stress of money is causing pain in your relationship with your spouse, friends, or family. It's for you if you're worried about your retirement portfolio or saving enough to send your children to college. It's for you if you're not sure whether you'll have enough money to carry you through a long, prosperous retirement. If you have more month than money, this fast is designed just for you. Or maybe you are already a good money manager, and now you're looking for ways to do better with the resources God has given you. This fast is for you even if you're doing just fine financially.

Whatever your financial situation, I challenge you to spend the next twenty-one days fasting.

Now this isn't going to be like any fast you've heard about or done before. Rather than eliminating only food or certain types of food, you're going to curtail your consumption in everything you *buy*.

The path to prosperity begins by breaking the yoke to buy and buy and then buy some more.

TAKE THE CLEANSING CHALLENGE

I'm inviting you to take a 21-day financial fast in which you will purchase only necessities. The fast is really about curbing the need to consume. It doesn't matter if you're a good steward or a spendthrift; all of us consume more than we need. We shop so much, we don't even stop to think about what we're buying. How many times have you gone to Walmart or Target with the intention of buying just a few things, but you ended up tossing more than a few things into your shopping cart? You get to the register, and a trip that should have cost you $20 ends up costing you $200.

If we all waited longer before making many of our purchases, we'd have more money. During this fast, don't even go window-shopping. Take shopping off your weekend to-do list.

For twenty-one days, you will exercise discipline in your use of credit. I want you to become acquainted again with the feel and limitations of cash. Using plastic in any form — credit card or debit card — makes it too easy to overspend. By breaking your attachment to credit and debit cards, I hope to help you realize how much you've come to rely on this plastic devil. You might protest, "But why give up my debit card? Isn't it the same as cash?" No, a debit card is not the same as cash because you can still spend more than you have. Despite how the banks have marketed debit cards, many people have found themselves hit with countless overdraft fees for swiping when they didn't have enough money in their bank accounts.

HOW TO USE THIS BOOK

This book includes twenty-one chapters — one for each day of the fast — and is divided into four parts:

    Part 1: Why a Financial Fast?

    Part 2: Fasting for a Better Financial Life

    Part 3: Fasting to Avoid Financial Drama

    Part 4: Fasting for Financial Peace

The chapters and parts build on each other to help you establish a strong foundation for financial peace and freedom. Part 1 lays the foundation of the fast. Whether you are a believer or not, prosperity just doesn't happen on its own. You have to make the right moves to prosper. But I also believe that God has the power to deliver financial freedom when you show Him you are a responsible steward over your money.

Part 2 is all about preparation, which includes addressing entitlement issues, learning to be content, budgeting, saving, and investing. If you're married and have children, it also means handling your money in a way that strengthens your relationship with your spouse and creates wealth for your heirs.

Part 3 is designed to help you get rid of the things that stand in the way of your prosperity — debt, credit, and greed. It also addresses one of the most pressing financial issues facing families, which is long-term care for oneself or for aging parents or relatives.

Part 4 focuses on the testimonies of people who have taken the 21-day fast and whose lives have been changed because of it. This section takes a look at what stands in your way of achieving financial peace.

The best way to read this book is one chapter a day. And even if that day's chapter doesn't directly apply to your life, find a takeaway that will help someone you know. Part of my mission is to multiply the success of this fast by equipping you to pass on what you learn to your family and friends.

Each chapter includes a daily assignment to help you apply what you're learning. In addition to reading time, you'll need to set aside some time each day to complete the assignment or assignments. In most cases you will be able to complete the tasks in one day, but some may take longer. For example, the assignment on Day 7 is to complete a budget, which is often a time-consuming task. Even if you can't finish it in a day, you can at least start the budgeting process by collecting all your debt, checking, savings, and income information — or get a head start and begin to gather those things now!

I've included lots of practical and inspirational tools to help you in this challenge. You will find several online tools at *www.michelle singletary.com*. In addition to things such as budgeting templates and a spending journal, the book features testimonies from people who have completed the fast, some several times. You may be surprised at the honesty of their self-assessments. No matter how strictly or loosely people followed the fast, everyone came away with some revelation that helped them manage their money better. Use their words as inspiration on the days you're tempted to cheat or actually cheat.

I want you to record your progress toward completing your assignments in a journal. Journaling is a wonderful way to have a conversation with yourself and with God. It also provides a record of your challenges and progress. In your journal, start off each day by indicating which day of the fast you are on.

This fast may be hard for you. Perhaps you have used shopping as a form of entertainment for so long, you can't even imagine going one weekend, let alone twenty-one days, without a trip to the mall. If you've become addicted to shopping or if you've been brainwashed to believe you can use credit wisely, prepare to be challenged!

Or maybe the fast won't be hard for you at all. You may already be a faithful steward over your money. And yet, I'm sure there are areas in which you can grow even more. Perhaps you're so tight with your money that you aren't as generous as you could be. Or maybe you're afraid to spend and enjoy your wealth because you fear poverty. This was a bond I had to break.

Wherever you fall on the financial spectrum — compulsive spender or good steward — you'll be surprised at how much more you can have when you follow God's blueprint for making, keeping, and giving away money. My prayer for you is that this 21-day financial fast will give you both the biblical principles and the practical tools to achieve the prosperity God promises.

Part One

WHY A FINANCIAL FAST?

Together, the first four chapters of this book focus on helping you understand what the financial fast is all about. Over the next four days, we'll consider the responsibilities that come with being rich, God's promise of prosperity, and the importance of things like generosity and tithing.

The chapters that follow build on the fasting theme and how depriving yourself will actually enrich your life. I want you to start thinking about your money and how often leaning on your own understanding can ultimately lead to making decisions about your money that aren't wise.

If you truly want to change the way you handle your money or view your finances, the Scripture references in this book can be your Lally column. In home construction, Lally columns are steel posts that provide important structural support to the house. The columns are typically found in a basement to support large, heavy overhead beams. So, too, does God's Word provide the structural support to achieve prosperity. Without that support, you might still achieve wealth, but you won't have the foundation you'll need in order to prosper with a purpose.

Twenty-One Days to Financial Freedom

---

21 Days to Go: Breaking Bonds

Main Point: We need to be set free from the bondage spending holds on our lives.

My Pledge: For the next twenty-one days, I will be on a spending diet. I will not shop for anything except necessities. I will not use my credit card. I will limit or eliminate the use of my debit card. I will use cash for purchases I make during the fast. In this way, I will strive to break the chains that keep me from achieving financial freedom.

"I *hated* the fast!"

That's what Terri, a federal government worker, said after she finished her first financial fast.

How's that for an opening line?

What you probably expected was a glowing testimony of someone who has gotten out of debt, or saved some amount of money for the first time in his or her life. I do have lots of those stories. In fact, one woman got rid of more than $100,000 in debt. You'll read more about her story later. But for now, I don't want to sugarcoat this process.

You need to know that this isn't going to be an easy journey. The

21-day financial fast is not a quick-fix, microwavable promise of instant prosperity. You will have to *work* for your financial freedom.

At times, you may want to quit. You may want to scream. You may even break the fast at some point during the twenty-one days. But no matter how many times you falter, make the commitment to get right back on track. Terri did. Here's more of her testimony:

> Trying to figure out what I could and could not spend money on was a nuisance. Every day I had conversations with myself that went something like this:
>
> **Me**: I'm hungry. What can I eat for dinner?
>
> **Other me**: Umm … Chinese food sounds good. Call that place that does takeout.
>
> **Me**: Oh shucks, I can't. I'm on that crazy financial fast. So what's in the house?
>
> **Other me**: But I'm too tired to cook.
>
> **Me**: Well, you promised you would stick to the fast. (All along, I'm hearing Michelle's voice in my head asking, "Is this a want or a need?")
>
> **Other me**: It's a need to eat. Ya think?
>
> **Me**: Yeah, but you don't *need* to buy food if you already have food at home.
>
> **Other me**: Oh, right.
>
> **Me**: Why did I agree to this?
>
> I'd search the fridge and cabinets for something to cook despite the fact that I was tired after a long commute from work. Every day for twenty-one days, I thought, "How am I gonna survive this?" On top of making dinner, I had to pack a lunch for the next day. Who feels like making lunch after cooking dinner?
>
> Trying to keep my family on track was another challenge, especially my husband, Larry, who is obsessed with going to the market. Prior to the financial fast, he never took a list to the store or stuck to a budget. He believed that because food is a necessity, it's okay to spend whatever you want at the market.

But all that work did pay off—literally. I saved $140 that month on lunch money alone.

The fast really made me think about how I spend.

Consider her words. The fast made her think about how she spends. When was the last time you really, truly thought about how you spend? When was the last time you looked at your budget, or even attempted to put one down on paper? When was the last time you looked at how much you give to your church or to charity?

This fast will make you reexamine your spending habits—and you may not like what you see. But you can't change that which you have not acknowledged. It's funny how I can sit down with someone, look at their budget, and immediately see what's been holding them back financially or why they are in so much debt. But they can't see it because they're too busy shopping or spending.

For example, Terri said her husband constantly exceeded their food budget. Through one-on-one counseling sessions and the fast, Larry realized why he overspent at the grocery store. As a child, he couldn't have certain foods because they were too expensive. The fast made Larry examine why he felt entitled to buy whatever he wanted when he went grocery shopping. Now that he's aware of what drives him to overspend at the market, he can rein in his spending and stay within their family's grocery budget.

You've probably heard that one definition of the word *crazy* is doing the same thing over and over again and expecting different results. Yet that's how many people handle their money, or should I say, mishandle their money. They never take the time to examine why they are spending the way they do. As a result, they can't rob Peter to pay Paul anymore because Peter is so broke, there isn't any money left to steal. Their finances are "tore up from the floor up"—meaning their finances are a wreck—but they persist in the same destructive habits. The problem for too many people is that they don't know their finances are jacked-up crazy.

WHAT IS A FINANCIAL FAST?

This isn't some gimmick. It is a God-inspired way for you to find financial freedom. The 21-day financial fast has been field-tested for several years in my home church, First Baptist Church of Glenarden in Prince George's County, Maryland.

I first introduced the fast as part of a volunteer program called Prosperity Partners Ministry. In this ministry, men and women who are good stewards over their personal finances (Senior Partners) become accountability partners for members who are having financial challenges (Junior Partners). As part of the ministry, all members — even those serving as Senior Partners — are asked to participate in the fast.

The concept of the fast is similar to the one the prophet Daniel took, in which he "ate no choice food; no meat or wine" and "used no lotions at all until the three weeks were over" (Dan. 10:3). Daniel fasted as a way to draw closer to God. Similarly, the principle of this financial fast is to deny your flesh so that you can become closer to God. Instead of relying on an emotional rush from shopping or pursuing the latest sale or discount, this fast will connect you to God. The rush you get from this fast is far better than snagging a pair of designer shoes on sale or upgrading to the latest electronic gadget. Fasting is an act of separating yourself from worldly pleasures. During this separation, and away from worldly temptation, you can begin to break the bonds that keep you broke.

During this fast you will not shop or use your credit cards for twenty-one days. For three weeks you must refrain from buying anything that is not a necessity. And by necessity, I mean the bare essentials, such as food and medicine.

During this fast you will refrain from going to the mall or retail stores to shop for clothes, shoes, jewelry, nonessential household items, or other stuff that creates a drag on your financial life (and clutters your home).

Even window-shopping is off limits. Browsing leads to temptation, which in turn can lead to buying something you don't really need.

No restaurant meals — fast food or otherwise. This includes buying breakfast or lunch at work. You can't stop for coffee. Make it at home instead. During the fast, forget going out to the movies.

You are not permitted to buy gifts or gift cards. I often get a lot of objections on this last rule. People are hesitant to show up empty-handed at a birthday party or wedding or any event where a gift is expected. So they ask if they can tell the birthday person or bride and groom that they'll get a gift for them at a later time. No.

You can't tell them you will buy a gift later. Don't promise to purchase a gift after the fast is over. Instead, use this opportunity to share with the honored person why you are fasting. Then find a way to bless them without purchasing something. This may be particularly hard if you have children. As any parent knows, birthday parties have become grand coronations with children expecting a table full of presents. We parents could help each other out by asking party guests on occasion *not* to bring gifts. At one party, in lieu of gifts for her child, the mother asked partygoers to bring books to exchange. I loved that idea. It took the focus off of receiving and put it on giving. "I really wanted him to know what fun is without expecting toys," the mother said.

Children's birthday parties have created a small but not insignificant dent in many household budgets. Besides, year after year of overindulgence at these parties can make it harder to teach your children about moderation later. Already we have an epidemic of overspending among adults. Perhaps this is how it starts.

One woman wrote to me that her five-year-old son was invited to two birthday parties during the fast, but she didn't allow him to go to the parties. However, that wasn't really necessary. While I loved that this mother was trying to stick to the fast, her son could have gone to the parties, only without a gift. "Just goes to show you how conditioned my mind was to spending money," Trina said. "I would have never thought about making a gift; I always purchase something instead."

It's okay to have fun on the fast; you just can't buy anything that isn't a necessity. If your child or teen is invited to a party during the fast, call the birthday child's parent or guardian and explain that your child would like to attend but the family is on a financial fast. Your child can make a gift from supplies you have at home or make a wonderful handmade birthday card.

I want you to internalize that you *can* celebrate life's greatest occasions without having to bring or receive a gift. I know this will be tough, but what in the world do most of us need anyway? What's most precious is the very thing money can't buy — time. So be creative. Find a way to give of yourself without spending. The purpose of the fast is to eliminate spending on absolutely *everything* that is not essential.

THE PERILS OF PLASTIC

Curtailing your consumption is just one part of the fast. The second part is eliminating the use of plastic, both credit and debit. There's a real danger in relying on credit even if you pay off your credit card bill every month. Paying with plastic just makes purchasing too easy. Swipe, and within seconds you can be mired in debt. Let's consider the example of purchasing a flat-screen television. If you had to stand at a cash register and count out bill after bill after bill to pay the hundreds, if not thousands, of dollars for a television, you certainly would contemplate whether the purchase made financial sense. You might even do some mental accounting to calculate what debts you could pay down or pay off instead. Plastic doesn't allow for that deliberation.

There are two kinds of credit card users — those who carry a balance and those who pay off their charges every month. Those who pay off their charges often assume they are in control of their credit card usage. After all, you have to admire the marketing might of credit card issuers. They have done a stellar job in persuading otherwise smart people that using plastic can come with no price. This group of convenience credit card users is convinced that they are pulling one over on the card companies. They point to the reward points they receive or the fact that they never, or seldom, pay any credit card interest. But I assure you there is a cost. You may be able to bear it, but there is an extra cost to using credit.

The banks know and studies have shown that even those of us who think we are using credit wisely are being duped. That's because when you use credit, you often spend more than you would if you use cash. Even if you don't pay interest on the money because you settle the bill before the next billing cycle, or if you collect a plane ticket or two as part of a credit card reward program, you're still spending more. That means the banks win and you lose.

In one study aimed at marketers, Greg Davies at Britain's Warwick University found that customers using credit cards spend more than those paying with cash or checks in purchasing situations that are otherwise identical in every other respect. Davies concludes that credit cards boost spending because of how our brains work. He found that credit cards reduce the pain of payment because we don't do the same mental accounting as we do when we pay with cash.

I know from experience that many people do not make the same purchases when they pay with plastic. This isn't just a feeling or anecdotal evidence. Researchers have found that people's willingness to purchase more products or services increases with the use of plastic.*

Over the years that the Prosperity Partners Ministry has conducted the financial fast, some business professional or small business

---

* In one study, participants were more willing to pay more for a restaurant meal when they used a credit card than when they used cash, according to findings by Priya Raghubir, PhD, of the Stern School of Business at New York University and Joydeep Srivastava, PhD, of the Robert H. Smith School of Business at the University of Maryland, College Park. The findings appeared in the September 2008 issue of the *Journal of Experimental Psychology: Applied*, published by the American Psychological Association.

entrepreneur inevitably objects to the no credit card rule, arguing that he or she may need to use credit during a work trip or for other business purposes. Generally speaking, during the fast, the rule about avoiding credit card use applies only to personal credit card use, but I would still ask you to consider if there is a way around using credit even for business reasons. Too many small business owners are unnecessarily deep in credit card debt.

You should also limit use of your debit card. If you must use it, limit your purchases to groceries and/or gas.

WHY LIMIT DEBIT CARD USE?

Through my work in Prosperity Partners, I've found that even debit card users, especially those without credit card debt — still whip out the plastic far too easily and spend more than they would if they were limited to using only cash. Many debit card users who have participated in the fast argue that they can't spend more than what's in their checking account; therefore, it's the same as cash. But that's not true. If it were true, the banks wouldn't have introduced overdraft protection, a common debit card feature that allows banks to rake in billions (yes, that's with a *b*) in fees.

About 90 percent of banks' consumer-fee income comes from overdraft and insufficient-funds charges. An overdraft study published in 2008 by the Federal Deposit Insurance Corporation found that at least 81 percent of banks allow overdrafts to take place at ATMs and through point-of-sale/debit transactions. An overwhelming majority of banks in the FDIC survey did not inform customers until after the transaction had been completed that they didn't have enough money in their bank account to cover their electronic transaction. Only about 8 percent of the financial institutions informed consumers that funds were insufficient before transactions were completed, thereby allowing them an opportunity to avoid a fee.

A debit card is a cousin to the credit card, and it poses a similar problem — it allows people to buy stuff with cash they really don't have. People are quick to swipe their debit card, only to learn later after getting an overdraft notice that they didn't have the cash in their bank account to back up the debit card purchase in the first place.

So you see, a debit card is not the same as using cash, since you can still spend more than you have in your bank account.

WHAT YOU CAN AND CAN'T DO DURING THE FAST

People find ways around the fast. I know that. I can't possibly come up with a list of all the don'ts that may violate the fast. For example, I tell people to only spend money on essential things. However, one person's essential is another's want. I can easily go twenty-one days without going to the hair salon. I'll throw my hair in a ponytail in a minute. Other women who've done the fast say if they went without visiting the hair salon, they would look a "hot mess" and possibly jeopardize their employment.

Here's a quick overview of what you can purchase during the financial fast:

- Essential items such as food and medication.
- Essential personal hygiene products.
- Essential clothing items that would be *required* for your job, such as pantyhose, work shirts, or a uniform. However, you should not buy clothing simply because you think you need a new outfit for work. If you're a professional and your work requires a certain standard of dress, then you should try to make do for the next twenty-one days with the clothes you already own.
- Essential items for your family. School supplies would fit under this category.
- Essential items for your home, such as cleaning products. Sheets, pillows, lamps, curtains, and so on are not essential unless the old ones are completely worn out or broken.

*Money cannot
purchase what
the heart desires.*

Chinese proverb

Again, I can't put together a definitive list of what you should and shouldn't buy during the fast. If a situation comes up that isn't on the list, keep in mind the spirit of the fast, which is to curtail your consumption. For example, let's say you're dating and your boyfriend (or girlfriend) volunteers to pick up the dining and entertainment tab during the twenty-one days. Should you accept the offer? You'd better say no thank you! It doesn't matter if your honey is paying. You would be violating the spirit of the fast, which is to stop participating in consumption. Instead, encourage your sweetheart to join you in the fast. Following is a nonexhaustive list of what you shouldn't do over the next three weeks:

- *Don't go to the mall.*
- *Don't window-shop.* A major objective of this fast is to stop using shopping as a form of entertainment. Just don't go there. Don't let your children go either. Don't let them "hang out" at the mall. Encourage your spouse to participate in the fast and ask him or her to avoid mall visits as well.
- *Don't shop online.* (Yes, Internet shopping counts!)
- *Don't browse through retail catalogs.* Put them away for the twenty-one days so they won't tempt you. In fact, when the Sunday paper comes, do you go straight for the retail circulars? Think about that. We shop in our minds even when we aren't shopping for real.
- *Don't buy meals outside the home.*
- *Don't go to the movies or to see a play or spend any money on entertainment.* You can go out and have fun, but you just can't spend any money while you're doing it. Instead, look for community programs that are free. Check with a local college to see if there's a free showing of a movie or a band or choir concert. Consider having a family game night. You can find ways to entertain yourself without using cash or credit.

- *Don't use plastic.* Use cash whenever possible. This fast is also about getting you connected to your cash. Please remember this: Even if you pay off your credit card bill every month, studies show you probably still spend 30 to 40 percent more when you use plastic, whether it's a credit card or debit card.
- *Don't allow yourself to buy things you know you shouldn't.* Be accountable to yourself. If overspending on your beautification (hair, manicures, pedicures, makeup purchases) is the yoke you know you have to break, then the answer is no, you can't get your hair (or nails) done during the fast.

Finally, let the Holy Spirit speak to you on what is and isn't allowed while you are fasting. You will know what's right if you listen to the Holy Spirit. And you'll know because you will have doubts about whether you should spend on a particular item or service.

I CAN SEE CLEARLY NOW

When you've removed yourself from constantly consuming, you can see more clearly how God is at work in your life. "When you take the focus off money, God handles your needs because you spend more time focusing on him," said Mellissa, a registered dental hygienist who found the fast brought her greater clarity about her finances.

Mellissa saved about $250 the first time she did the fast, and that was just by eliminating basic "snackage" such as morning breakfast treats and trips to fast food restaurants. "I saw things in my home I didn't need and returned them, [thus] reducing my credit card debt," she said. "I also learned that if you look around the house at what you already have, twenty-one days of no shopping is a walk in the park."

Remember Terri, who said she initially hated the fast? She and her husband ended up making major changes in how they handled their money. And those changes came in very handy when Larry lost his job.

"Although we didn't have a lot of savings for such an emergency, we had some," Terri said. "More importantly, we had a system developed out of the fast that allowed us to spend differently, more wisely within our budget. We learned how to readjust the budget based on the income coming in. The job loss set us back some for things like our son's college fund, but our primary expenses were still covered. We didn't freak out. We still tithed and saved."

FIVE FASTING TIPS

Here are five things you can do to make your fast a thumbs-up success:

1. **Get a journal**. For the purposes of the fast, consider it an essential need! Every day, write down your feelings, fears, or frustrations about your finances. You will primarily use the journal to record your progress in completing your daily assignments at the end of every chapter, but feel free to record your thoughts and feelings along the way.

2. **Review your progress**. After the fast is over, review your journal notes to see what growth or insights you have had. It will also help you to be accountable as you keep track of the assignments you actually complete. Try to be as specific as possible when you record your thoughts and emotions so that they'll make sense to you when you read them several days or weeks from now. If it helps you to see an example of a journal entry, I've included a sample in the appendix (page 244).

3. **Get a highlighter**. Use the highlighter to mark the particular biblical passages mentioned throughout the chapters that speak to you about your individual issues. Include your thoughts and questions about these passages in your journal.

4. **Get an accountability partner**. I highly recommend you do the fast with someone else. You may need help making sure you follow the fast. If you like, make it a family affair, or start a fasting group at your church or at your job. The point is to find a person

or a group of people who will support you and help hold you accountable during the fast. You each should get your own book.

5. Start each day with the "P-A-Y" regimen.

Pray before you read each chapter. Ask God to open your mind and your heart and reveal to you how to better handle your finances.

Act on the pledge listed at the start of each chapter. The financial fast won't change your finances long-term if you don't implement the things I ask you to do. For example, on Day 7, "The Benefits of Budgeting," I ask you to create a budget. Just do it. If the budget is already in your head, put it down on paper. The point of a budget is to account for all the money coming into and going out of your household. When you budget well, every penny has a purpose!

Yield to God's will, not your own. Often people find themselves in financial trouble because they've acted on their own accord instead of waiting on the Lord. You may want to meditate on this Scripture for the first day of the fast: "He guides the humble in what is right and teaches them his way" (Ps. 25:9). Yielding is very important. You won't make it through this fast without surrendering yourself to the will of God. Trust that he will help you become a better steward over your money. Believe in your heart that God wants you to prosper.

TESTIMONY TIME: *Day 1*

The financial fast was truly a foreign concept to me. Even though I wasn't supposed to spend, I often found myself purchasing things like books and magazines. But by paying attention to what I spent, I found out that I was spending anywhere from $500 to $1,000 a year on books, magazines, CDs, DVDs, and other media items.

It was my heart's desire to stay on track for the whole month, but of course I fell off the wagon on occasion. I tried to incorporate "mess-up days" into my financial fast for the days I spent money, but God began to convict me that this was an excuse to justify spending. God said, "Why have a 21-day financial fast with built-in 'mess-up days'?"

I thank God that spending is no longer my yoke. Now I spend when there is a need. I wait until everything is used up before purchasing and hoarding items in my home.

Juanita

So are you ready for the challenge? Are you ready to break through the wickedness that has a stranglehold on your finances, preventing you from increasing your net worth? Make the commitment today to untie the yoke that keeps you financially oppressed. Or, fast to become even better at handling your money. Whatever your situation, embark on this fast to put the focus back on God and away from what you have or don't have.

It's time to go to God in prayer. It's time to fast.

DAILY ASSIGNMENT

Make a list of any potential obstacles that may prevent you from sticking to the fast and then decide how to eliminate them. For example, instead of putting your credit cards in a drawer or file cabinet, freeze them. Yes, that's what I said. Put the cards in the freezer. That's what one person did so that she wouldn't be tempted to use her cards. If you are a shopaholic, you may need to change your driving pattern so that you don't go near your favorite shopping places.

Take this pledge and then sign your name on the line below:

"I promise to follow the 21-day financial fast so that I may put myself on the path of prosperity and financial freedom."

A Promise of Prosperity

20 Days to Go: God Will Provide

Main Point: God promises prosperity.

My Pledge: To find the key to wealth, I have to understand that prosperity comes with conditions. I must follow God's will and Word for my life.

After her husband announced he wanted a divorce, Juanita was devastated. Divorce tears a family apart, both spiritually and financially.

Juanita came to a presentation I was giving at church and asked how she could turn her financial life around. Still living in a home she could no longer afford without her husband's income, she was broken and beaten down.

"What do we do when our mate walks out on us leaving us with the mortgage and more debt than we can imagine?" Juanita asked during the session. "I am more than $100,000 in debt."

After she asked the question, the room was silent, except for a few whispers of "Lord, have mercy."

I've heard this sort of testimony more times than I can count. I've heard situations that are completely desperate. What the person is really asking for is a miracle. But since only God can deliver miracles, I answered Juanita with the best solution for her situation.

"Get a roommate," I told her.

Juanita looked at me as if I were crazy. The murmurs from people in the audience told me they, like Juanita, felt that I had given her bad advice. I knew they thought I wasn't being sensitive to her plight. I could imagine them thinking, *Is that all you have to offer this poor woman?* Even Juanita stared at me with a look that said, *I would cuss you out, but we're in church!*

I'm amazed at how those in need often refuse to move out of their comfort zones to bring peace into their lives. Juanita needed a roommate to help with her mortgage payments. I wasn't going to bail her out with cash, and neither were the people in that audience. She couldn't get a second job because she was already overworked. She had cut out from her budget all the expenses that she could. Temporarily getting a roommate was the only way to get some financial breathing room in her budget.

People often want God to fulfill his promise of prosperity, but they don't want to change. They don't want to make the hard choices, which might mean giving up cable TV or their cell phone or eating out, or getting a roommate if the mortgage or rent is too much for them to bear alone. Or moving — even with a child or children — to someone else's home.

Shortly after that encounter with Juanita I proposed the idea for Prosperity Partners, and then the 21-day fast. Juanita was one of the first participants. She committed to the fast as if she were fighting for her life. In many ways, she was. In the end, she took my advice and got a roommate.

"Three roommates later, God blessed me exceedingly and abundantly above all that I can ask or think," Juanita wrote to me after going through her third 21-day fast. Juanita would do the fast sometimes twice a year. It helped her to become 100 percent debt free!

Juanita initially balked at getting a roommate because she didn't want to share her space. She was also too proud to admit she couldn't handle all the expenses by herself. But when she realized that God was in fact just waiting for her to call on him, she changed. She began to budget and bring some order into her financial life.

Prosperity is only an instrument to be used, not a deity to be worshipped.

Calvin Coolidge

"I have learned that when our finances are in order, every aspect of our lives is in order as well," she said. "Our finances are the foundation on which everything else is based."

MONEY MATTERS

Juanita learned that money does matter. King Solomon said as much when he wrote, "Money is the answer for everything" (Eccl. 10:19). To live in this world, you need money. Without money you can't buy a home or a car, send your children to college, or retire with dignity.

Throughout the Old and New Testaments God promises that those who follow his Word will prosper. Jesus said in John 10:10, "I have come that they may have life, and have it to the full." Of course, in many of those Scriptures God is talking about spiritual wealth. However, on earth we need money to survive. So God's promise for prosperity comes with a condition.

The condition is that we have to put God first in all things. As it says in Matthew 6:33, "But seek first his kingdom and his righteousness, and all these things will be given to you as well."

The question becomes, "How can we put God first if we don't know him or have a relationship with him?" If we don't have a relationship with him, we won't lean on him when we have lean times. Instead, we'll lean on our own understanding, which usually leads us in the wrong direction and results in our losing even more money.

How often do you find yourself in financial difficulty, and instead of calling on God to help and then waiting patiently for an answer, you do something that ends up making things worse? For example, an alarming number of people turn to payday lenders to bail them out when money gets tight. Payday loans are small loans a borrower promises to repay out of his or her next paycheck, typically within two weeks. I'm troubled by these loans because when the fees are annualized, they often amount to triple-digit interest rates — even more than 1,000 percent interest in many cases.

Some people even pledge their automobiles to get a loan. Like payday loans, car-title loans are marketed as small emergency loans to people who own their cars or trucks outright. A typical car-title loan has a triple-digit annual interest rate, requires repayment within one month, and is usually made for much less than the value of the car. In a title loan transaction, you keep your car, and the lender keeps the title as security for repayment of the loan. If you fail to repay the loan, you run the risk of losing your car.

Using a credit card to buy things you can't pay off the next month is bad enough, but borrowing against your next paycheck or your car is an incredibly risky and unwise financial move. It's a move made by desperate people who probably didn't turn to God for help. The Bible says we should honor our word and pay our debts, yet people charge on their credit cards with no idea how they are going to pay it off. Scripture repeatedly warns us to stay out of debt, and yet we pile it on our lives like a heap of mashed potatoes.

The pursuit of prosperity — or what passes for prosperity — often leads us away from God. For example, so they can save money, some Christian women and men live together. They know that cohabitation outside of marriage is against God's plan. But they do it anyway so they can have more.

All of these actions are done not with God in mind but with our own selfish intentions. And then we wonder why we're broke. God can't fulfill his promise if we don't hold up our end of the bargain.

BROKEN COMMANDMENTS

On this second day of the fast I want you to think about — and then write about in your journal — all the things you do or have done that have prevented you from being prosperous. Which of God's commandments have you broken that have literally left you broke? Or which commandment(s) did you ignore that robbed you of financial peace? Using five of the Ten Commandments, let me give you some examples of what I've seen people do, and then you'll have an opportunity at the end of the chapter in your daily assignment to write your own responses in your journal.

God says: "Remember the Sabbath day by keeping it holy" (Ex. 20:8).

What I've seen: I attend a large church with thousands of members. Before we built a new sanctuary, many of us had to worship in overflow rooms set up with big-screen televisions. To get a seat in the main sanctuary, you had to arrive not just on time, but very early before service started. My family doesn't do early. So we worshiped almost all the time in the overflow areas. In fact, my pastor called us "OR" for "overflow regulars." But can you guess the one time we were able to get a seat in the main sanctuary? The last Sunday before Christmas! We could get a seat during the holidays because so many members skipped the weekend service to go shopping. How sad that shopping for these folks was more important than celebrating the birth of Christ. And I know many of the people who chose to shop rather than hold the Sabbath sacred couldn't afford what they were buying anyway.

God says: "Honor your father and your mother" (Ex. 20:12).

What I've seen: I often get letters from parents who are beside themselves and nearly broke trying to bail out their "trifling" adult children. These adults sometimes return home to live off their parents. There is even a term for this trend — the Boomerang Generation.

The Boomerang Generation mostly includes recent college graduates, but others are coming back to their parents' homes because they failed to handle their money wisely. Then they dishonor their parents by continuing to manage their finances recklessly. With no rent, utilities, or even food bills to pay, they feel free to spend wildly. I understand

and even recommend that some adults move back home to get their financial bearings if things get tough. It makes economic sense for a college graduate with lots of student loan debt to move back home in an effort to pay off or at least pay down that debt. However, moving back home is not a license to take advantage of your parents.

God says: "You shall not commit adultery" (Ex. 20:14).

What I've seen: I wonder if the folks who commit adultery realize the high price they pay for their indiscretions. I've had to help a number of women whose husbands have abandoned their families to chase after other women. Aside from the sexual immorality of adultery, this sin can ruin a family financially and increase the cost to society. Divorce costs US taxpayers $112 billion each year, according to one study commissioned by four groups — Institute for American Values, Georgia Family Council, Institute for Marriage, and Public Policy Families Northwest. The estimate includes the cost of federal, state, and local government social service programs. Another study found that after divorce, women experience a 27 percent decline in their standard of living.

God says: "You shall not steal" (Ex. 20:15).

What I've seen: Far too many people, Christians included, believe there's nothing wrong with *not* reporting all their income to the Internal Revenue Service. According to a survey conducted for *lawyers.com*, more than one in ten Americans think it's acceptable to cheat on their taxes. Cheating on your taxes is the same as stealing.

God says: "You shall not covet your neighbor's house. You shall not covet your neighbor's wife, or his male or female servant, his ox or donkey, or anything that belongs to your neighbor" (Ex. 20:17).

What I've seen: Many people break this commandment. They want so badly what others have. In part, it is coveting or desiring what others have that has caused many people to buy homes they couldn't afford. The Joneses had a big house, so they wanted one too.

We give in to the covetous nature of our children as well. Seriously, who in their right mind would buy their children sneakers that cost $100 or more and not have a penny saved up for that child's college education? And yet I see it all the time. The kid wants the sneakers because that's what the other kids have, and the parent goes right along with what their kid wants.

Why do so many children have cell phones? Because their friends have a cell phone and they nag their parents for one. Isn't that coveting?

If you want God's promised prosperity, you have to believe he will supply all your needs. The Bible teaches that God "will meet all your needs according to the riches of his glory in Christ Jesus" (Phil. 4:19). That's a promise you can rely on.

Notice the intentional use of the word *needs*, not *wants*. People are getting into trouble because they want something so much they can't wait to save up for it. They can't wait for God to allow it to come into their lives, or they just go into debt to get it.

If you want God's promise of prosperity, you also have to act in ways that are consistent with God's principles so you are prepared to receive his riches.

TESTIMONY TIME: *Day 2*

My aha moment came when I said to Michelle that I felt like a failure because I couldn't afford to buy a house. I just couldn't understand how, at my age and with my education and salary, I still couldn't afford to own my own home. I thought the American Dream was to go to college, get a good job, get married, have kids, and buy your own home. Well, I knew the husband wasn't coming any time soon, so I thought I could alter the dream a little and go for home ownership on my own. But the market in my area makes buying a house cost prohibitive. However, so many others I knew were purchasing homes. I felt ashamed and embarrassed because I was just renting. When I told Michelle how I felt, she looked at me and said, "You are not a failure." She said home ownership is only one way to build wealth, and while it is a good thing, it's not for everyone. After that I finally accepted that it was okay I had not yet bought a home. Thank you for freeing me from feelings of failure. You have definitely been a blessing to me and my savings account.

Cassandra

DAILY ASSIGNMENT

Listed below are the Ten Commandments. As you review each one, ask yourself these questions: "Have I broken this commandment in ways that have left me broke? Have I ignored a commandment and been robbed of financial peace?" After each commandment are some additional questions to consider. You don't have to answer all the questions, but read through and see which ones most apply to you. Write your responses in your journal.

"You shall have no other gods before me" (Ex. 20:3). *Think of ways in which money may have become your god.*

"You shall not make for yourself an image in the form of anything in heaven above or on the earth beneath or in the waters below. You shall not bow down to them or worship them" (Ex. 20:4 – 5). *Recall some of the purchases you've made over the last week. Which purchases represent things you trusted God to provide for you? Which represent chasing after wealth?*

"You shall not misuse the name of the LORD your God" (Ex. 20:7). *List at least one time in which you cursed God for your not having the things you want. How did that impact your relationship with God?*

"Remember the Sabbath day by keeping it holy" (Ex. 20:8). *How often have you skipped going to church to go shopping? Do you* **choose** *to work on the Sabbath so that you can earn more money to buy more things you don't need? How much richer might your life be (in nonmaterial ways) if you had a true Sabbath every week — a day devoted completely to rest?*

"Honor your father and your mother" (Ex. 20:12). *Think back and list the times (at least once if applicable) when you would have helped your parents financially but you couldn't because you had mismanaged your money.*

"You shall not murder" (Ex. 20:13). *Recall and write down as many times as you can remember when you said something like, "I would kill for that house." Yes, it's just an expression, but words do matter.*

"You shall not commit adultery" (Ex. 20:14). *Whether or not you have been on either side of adultery, write down the financial impact it can have on a family.*

"You shall not steal" (Ex. 20:15). *Write down any incident where you may have stolen something. For example, if you habitually show up late or waste time on the job, how would you feel if you were the boss?*

"You shall not give false testimony against your neighbor" (Ex. 20:16). *Think back and write about any time you've bad-mouthed a coworker in hopes of gaining favor with your supervisor. Have you sabotaged someone's career so you could get ahead and earn more money? If so, how do you feel about that now?*

"You shall not covet your neighbor's house. You shall not covet your neighbor's wife, or his male or female servant, his ox or donkey, or anything that belongs to your neighbor" (Ex. 20:17). *In the last month, has there been any time when you coveted someone else's possessions? Why do you think you want what that person has?*

God's Generosity

19 Days to Go: Cheerful Giving

Main Point: To whom much is given, much is required.

My Pledge: I will identify someone — a friend, family member, neighbor, or coworker — who needs help either with cash (I can afford to give away) or my time. I will use God's generosity toward me as an example of how to be generous to others. As I prosper, I will share my wealth with others.

During one of my online discussions for the *Washington Post*, I received the following comment from a chat participant:

> In a few situations, you have asked people with economic issues to consider moving in with their parents or some other relative. Please don't encourage people too much in this regard. In the last seven months, I have had requests from three relatives to move in because they mismanaged their finances and now can't afford to live on their own. I have refused them because I don't need to take on their issues. I am careful with my money because I don't want to depend on roommates. Please advise people to find other ways to reduce their expenses — a smaller house or apartment, a second job, or even

finding a roommate. But do not encourage them to mooch off their relatives. That is not a real solution.

I read that statement and felt sorry for this person. Imagine if everyone were so selfish. Imagine if God said, "You know what, you've been so triflin' I'm not going to be generous and help you out of yet another jam that you got yourself into."

It's so easy to refuse to help others when you feel they were irresponsible. It's tempting to pass judgment and think you've done better for yourself on your own. But don't be so arrogant to think you got where you are by your own actions. Contrary to popular wisdom, you can't pull yourself up by your own bootstraps. Whether you acknowledge it or not, you had help.

I'm grateful God doesn't use the same measure as humans do when it comes to granting grace. If you are allowed to prosper, be generous to others — even if it means helping those who haven't been as responsible as they should have been.

If you're still inclined to agree with the chat participant, consider the following few words that describe what her remarks reveal about her character:

Self-righteous: "They mismanaged their finances and now can't afford to live on their own."

Self-centered: "I have refused them because I don't need to take on their issues."

Self-absorbed: "I am careful with my money."

It's all about "self" for this person. Where's the compassion for her relatives? Where's the charity? Where's the self-realization that God gives us the power to prosper but with the proviso that we help our family and others? Where's the recognition that one day she may be in need? Do you think any of those relatives she turned away will rush to her aid if or when she falls down?

THE RESPONSIBILITIES OF PROSPERITY

Let me ask you this: Why do you want to prosper?

I ask this question because you need to understand that this financial fast isn't about showing you how to save, budget, or get out of debt so you can accumulate more things. It's not all about you. Certainly, my goal is to put you in a position where you have financial security, but I also want you to prosper so that you can lift up someone else. On Day 3 of this fast I want you to really consider the responsibilities that come with being prosperous.

At the day of reckoning, how will you answer our Lord when he asks how you treated the poor or your neighbor or your family when they were in need? When he asks how you used the resources he gave to you to serve others, will you be able to say that you generously helped others?

At times I have taken in relatives. And yes, they were in financial trouble at least in part due to their own fault. But I took them in anyway. Why purchase a house and save money if you aren't willing to help those who fall or who are imperfect with their finances?

My nephew, Tom, was fresh out of high school with no job prospects, so my husband and I told him he could live with us until he could manage to live on his own. My nephew will admit to this day that he was triflin'. His idea of looking for a job was to get up at about 10 or 11 a.m., search the newspaper classified ads, and declare he couldn't find work. Despite his unenthusiastic efforts to find a job, I didn't throw him out. My husband and I used the opportunity to teach him how to provide for himself. We began charging him rent even while he was unemployed. By the time he had racked up a few hundred dollars in overdue rent, he hustled to get a job. We made him contribute to the food budget. We made him budget and show us his bank statement to prove he was saving to get his own place. In about a year, my nephew was ready to move out. I was so proud when he showed me his budget. On the piece of notebook paper he had even scratched out cable when he realized he couldn't afford it. He now owns his own home.

Of course, you have to be careful about whom and how you help. You have to be careful about whom you take into your home. I wouldn't take in someone who is abusive or using drugs. But being triflin' with your money doesn't get you knocked off my help list.

Contrast the earlier note I received from the online chat participant with Adrienne's testimony below. A single mother, Adrienne went through the 21-day fast and learned to save so well that she was eventually able to help a childhood friend who needed a place to live after she became pregnant.

TESTIMONY TIME: *Day 3*

The financial fast has had a profound effect on the way I spend my money. Prior to participating in the financial fast, I thought I was supposed to spend my entire paycheck until the money was gone.

I am now able to tithe fully every month plus give an offering. I was even able to contribute $1,000 to our church building fund and began sponsoring a child through World Vision. And most significantly, when I received a call from a childhood friend in a desperate situation, I invited her to move in with me. I supported her financially through the last seven months of her pregnancy and then supported her and her baby for another seven months before she moved out.

The principles I learned through the financial fast helped me understand how to live below my means and save aggressively for both planned and unplanned needs in the future.

Adrienne

What Adrienne did reminds me of the hospitality and generosity of the Old Testament Shunammite woman who lived in the town of Shunem. We don't even know her name, but we know she was wealthy and helped the prophet Elisha, who at first was a stranger to her (2 Kings 4:8 – 37). The Shunammite woman and her husband dedicated a special room in their home to Elisha. Like the Shunammite woman, Adrienne saw a need and met it. She was able to immediately use her newfound prosperity to help someone else. She could have easily bought a new car or treated herself to a vacation. In fact, Adrienne had planned to take a trip to the Caribbean to celebrate her thirtieth birthday. Instead she chose to stay home, pay off some debts, and help a new single mother.

If you are in a position to help someone, then help them. I don't mean that you should enable people to continue making bad money decisions. But be mindful of what Scripture teaches about managing the resources God gives us: "From everyone who has been given much, much will be demanded; and from the one who has been entrusted with much, much more will be asked" (Luke 12:48). After all, didn't Jesus make the ultimate sacrifice? Isn't he the example of extreme generosity? He gave his life so that we could live ours abundantly. "For you know the grace of our Lord Jesus Christ, that though he was rich, yet for your sake he became poor, so that you through his poverty might become rich" (2 Cor. 8:9).

I've seen such great generosity that I can't help but feel obligated to give and give generously. Had it not been for my grandmother taking me in, I have no idea where I would be today. Big Mama was about fourteen years away from retirement when she took me in, along with my four siblings, who were between the ages of two and eight. She would have had more money for retirement had she not raised us. She could have had more of a lot of things. Yet, she gave what she had so that we could live as comfortably as she could afford. Perhaps of all the concepts in this book, this one is the most important. What I'm laying out for you isn't a plan to prosper for selfish gain. It's a blueprint to share your riches so that others may prosper too.

THE MISER'S MONEY

Are you a miser?

Do you cling to your money because you are afraid of not having enough? Have you told yourself you can't tithe or give to charity or even help out your extended family because if you part with your money, you'll end up broke? Are you making your family miserable with your cheapness?

If you answered yes to these questions, then I'm sorry to tell you that you're not frugal—you're a miser. And there is a big difference between the two. When you are frugal, you try to wisely use the money God has provided. But a miser is something else altogether. Misers use money for their own selfish good. They hoard. Hoarders have an unhealthy amount of fear about not having enough.

Hoarders remind me of Gizmo, the poodle mix I adopted from an animal shelter. The shelter suspected that Gizmo's former owners dumped him on the street after finding out he had a heart problem. I paid for the operation to fix the dog's heart (that's another story), and he lived for many years. But there was one thing from Gizmo's past that he could never shake. He always hid food. I would lift a pillow or rug and find scraps of dog food. No matter how much I fed him, he stashed chunks of food around the house. It was sad, really. Even though he no longer had to scrounge for food, he remained fearful that he might go hungry.

I think misers are haunted by the same fears that haunted Gizmo. Some are just greedy, but many are probably scared of not having enough, so they drive their families crazy with their miserly ways. That's not a healthy place to be. God says he will provide and we have to believe that.

You cannot prosper and be miserly. And by that, I don't mean you can't accumulate money. You can. But you won't enjoy the grace and prosperity God has for you. Misers are often unhappy because they are so fearful; thus they can't enjoy their financial blessings. You can have earthly riches, but you can still be poor spiritually. I have a relative who retired with lots of money, but she was so miserly that few relatives wanted to visit her. She lived a lonely existence worrying about her money.

In the name of frugality, some misers cheat because they reason

When a sparrow sips in the river, the water doesn't recede. Giving charity does not deplete wealth.

Punjabi proverb

that it "saves" them money. Here's a practical example: Taking more packets of condiments than you need at a fast food restaurant so you can use them later is stealing. Purchasing an outfit with the intention of wearing it to an event and then returning it to the store after the event is over is deceitful. Not returning the extra money a cashier gives you by accident is dishonest.

When my family and I were vacationing in Hilton Head, South Carolina, we decided to take a day trip to Savannah, Georgia, to shop along the waterfront. We went in and out of several stores during the day, mostly just window-shopping. Near dusk, we made the trek back to our car. As we began to load our kids and things into the car, we discovered a hat we had not purchased in my then two-year-old son's stroller. Clearly the tot had picked up the hat unbeknownst to any of us. So we had to get the kids out of their car seats and take the long walk back to the store to return the hat.

Well, we got back to the car and again began to put my son and his sister in their car seats. As I was looking through my son's diaper bag, I discovered another item he had taken from another store. It was a cassette tape with the same music we would play for him at home. He must have thought it was his tape, so he took it and put it in his diaper bag.

We had to unload the children again (they were too small to leave in the car) and return the tape.

On the third trip back to the car, a family friend vacationing with us said, "Don't look in that bag again!"

But you know, if I had found another item, I would have returned it even though I was bone tired of walking there and back along the hilly, cobblestone waterfront.

On numerous shopping trips I've been given too much change from a cashier during the checkout process. Or I've realized once I left the store that the clerk neglected to ring up an item. Each time I've pointed out the mistake to the clerk or returned the items to the store to have them properly rung up. I've heard some people say these mistakes are gifts from heaven. I don't think so. I think they're a test. The question is, did you pass or fail when you were tested?

I've told you these stories as examples of how a miserly heart cheats in the name of frugality. It is not honorable to be a miser. It's not good for your family relations either. Often the children of misers grow up to be spendthrifts — people who spend wastefully — because they felt so unnecessarily deprived during their youth. Or as you will see in the next section, children of misers have no shame in living off their parents as adults.

GENERATIONAL GENEROSITY GONE ASTRAY

You can't prosper by piggybacking on your parents' prosperity.

Too often adult children lean on their parents to bail them out, counting on their generosity to help them survive. Is that you? Are you constantly begging your parents or older relatives for a handout?

My pastor gave a message one Sunday in which he declared that adult children should regularly set aside money in their budgets to take care of their elderly parents. There were only a few "amens." Clearly he had stepped on some toes.

I regularly hear from retired seniors who are tapping into their savings to help grown children who are in trouble. Some grandparents are helping pay the expenses for grandchildren. And these are not for grandchildren whose parents have abandoned them or otherwise have some issues. These children are being raised in comfortable middle-class, two-parent, two-income households.

If you are retired and have amassed a great deal of money and want to help your adult children, who I am to criticize such generosity? But I'm concerned about the number of letters and emails I get from financially stressed-out seniors who complain about the constant requests for money from adult children with good jobs and decent incomes.

In a survey for the American Savings Education Council and AARP, 25 percent of respondents ages twenty-eight to thirty-nine said they had received financial support from friends or family in the past year. There are too many grown folks all too willing to ask for money from their aging parents. Having been raised by my grandmother, I vowed that I would help take care of her until the day she died. After I graduated, I paid my grandmother's property taxes every year (since she had already paid off her home). I regularly gave Big Mama money for groceries. My grandmother had managed her money well so she didn't really need the money. I just wanted to help out so that she wouldn't worry about outliving her savings.

Big Mama never asked for a penny. But I built a cushion into my monthly budget to take care of the woman who raised me from the time I was four years old. I never took a dollar from her after I began working full-time. If you are a parent of young children and you want your adult kids to have the financial muscle to care for you as you age, then teach them now how to handle their money. Encourage them to do the 21-day fast. Show them how to be generous.

I'm hoping this fast will help end generational poverty. I'm praying that it will show you God is able to bless you abundantly, so that when you have all you need, you can reach back and pull others up financially.

TESTIMONY TIME: *Day 3*

I have been in the church pretty much all of my life. I was taught about fasting at an early age and did so diligently. We always fasted from food and sometimes food and liquids. However, I had never engaged in a financial fast.

It was the most difficult thing I have ever done. It made me face the spoiled part of me that I didn't want to deal with, and it made me be more accountable with how I spent money. Because I do okay financially, I really had to discipline myself because spending would not break my budget.

I am a hat person. The financial fast broke what I thought was a "need" to buy hats. I learned I could do without. I also learned that if I waited on the Lord, he would allow people to bless me. People gave me hats or I was given gift certificates. It was almost two years from my first financial fast before I purchased a hat. That was a real accomplishment for me.

I learned that God wants to use me to be a blessing to others, as opposed to lavishing myself with things all the time. So yes, I try to make sure that I make my money count in the kingdom!

To sum it up: Discipline + Self-denial = Cents for the Kingdom!

Min. Garner

DAILY ASSIGNMENT

Think of at least one person who could use some help financially. For example, perhaps there is someone you know struggling to purchase groceries. Could you pick up some extra grocery items for them when you do your shopping? If you can't afford to help someone with cash, how else might you ease their financial burden? Perhaps you could offer to babysit for an evening. Maybe you know a neighbor whose car is being repaired or has been repossessed. Offer to drive the person on a few errands or take them to work for a week free of charge.

Tithing Today

18 Days to Go: First Fruits

Main Point: Tithing is still applicable today.

My Pledge: I will commit to tithing or recommit to continue tithing.

On Sundays my grandmother, Big Mama, would put just a few dollars in the collection plate. Once when the minister preached about tithing, Big Mama clutched her purse closer and pursed her lips.

"You ain't getting another penny from me," she whispered to herself.

My grandmother's comment is the first memory I have about tithing. The word *tithe* means a tenth part, or 10 percent. Many cultures and religions encourage faithful giving. For those who believe in tithing, it means paying that 10 percent first — before any bills are paid. I should also point out that giving an offering is different from paying your tithe. An offering is what you give above and beyond your tithe. For example, you might give an offering for your church's building fund.

I understood my grandmother's thinking about tithing. After raising her own children, she raised me and my four brothers and

sisters. She didn't make much as a nurse's assistant, and my grandfather, although quiet and gentle, often spent his paydays drinking up
most of his paycheck in the local bars.

Big Mama was never sure how much of my grandfather's money
would make it home, so she didn't tithe, or for that matter, give much
in the way of offerings. She didn't teach me to tithe. In fact, what she
passed on to me was a fear of not having enough. So for the longest
time I didn't tithe. I was too scared. When you have fears of being
homeless and pushing a grocery cart around town, tithing is hardly
something you embrace.

Often when you grow up poor or low income, you worry so much
about having enough money that you may not give as much as you
could or should. That was my story. As a result, I was always tor-
mented about tithing. My heart was willing but my head kept telling
me there were bills to pay.

After much prayer and with the help of my husband, I realized
that my fears about tithing were grounded in my lack of faith. So my
husband and I decided to begin tithing — on our gross income, not
net. We decided to trust that what we paid in the way of our tithes
was not going to deplete what we needed for our family.

And it hasn't.

Maybe you aren't tithing because you're concerned the money
isn't going to be used wisely. Then do some due diligence. Check to
make sure your church or religious organization is properly using the
tithes it receives.

More often than not people want to tithe but can't see how to do
it because they're already struggling. So practically, how do you tithe?

You begin tithing by building it into your budget. It has to come
first. If you tithe after everyone else is paid, there won't be any left
over to give back to God. I say "give back" because it's God's money
in the first place. Tithing forces you (or it should) to look at your
entire financial picture. It helps you become a better steward over
your money. There's no question that tithing can be tough. But with

careful budgeting you can develop a habit of giving that will enrich your life. (You'll learn more about budgeting and do some budgeting exercises on Day 7).

Now I'm not suggesting you let your mortgage or monthly car payment go unpaid in order to tithe. You should not shirk your other financial obligations in order to tithe. Those debts should be honored and paid accordingly. However, to do it all you have to become dogmatic about watching your expenses. That may mean making some different life choices. For example, if your mortgage is too heavy, you may need to get a roommate, or you may need to buy a used car instead of a new one. You may even need to put away your credit cards permanently. In the end, if you commit to tithing, you also need to commit to managing your money better so you won't have to pull back from tithing when times get tough.

TESTIMONY TIME: *Day 4*

I learned in the fast to never sacrifice the tithe. God will not only take care of you but reward you.

Mellissa

TORMENTED ABOUT TITHING

There are some who believe that Christians have been relieved of their obligation to tithe because there is no specific directive from Jesus in the New Testament to tithe. While Jesus never directly said we should tithe, neither did he say we should stop. What he did say is this, "Do not think that I have come to abolish the Law or the Prophets; I have not come to abolish them but to fulfill them" (Matt. 5:17). Why would tithing be abolished when it is a practice that helps support your local church?

Jesus did speak of tithing and endorsed it in a rebuke of the religious leaders of his day: "Woe to you, teachers of the law and Pharisees, you hypocrites! You give a tenth of your spices — mint, dill and cumin. But you have neglected the more important matters of the law — justice, mercy and faithfulness. You should have practiced the latter, without neglecting the former" (Matt. 23:23). Christ confirms the practice of tithing — "you give a tenth" — and reinforces it by saying, "without neglecting the former." The former he refers to is giving a tenth or tithing.

People will argue that tithing was part of the law given by Moses and that we are no longer under that law. But tithing was established long before the law was given to Moses. I'm not a biblical scholar or a minister, so I'm not going to debate doctrine on this issue. You're grown and you are going to do what you want anyway. Giving is always a personal choice, so no one can make you tithe. If you are looking for a way out of rendering a tenth of your income, you'll find it. There are plenty of websites, blogs, theories, and even theologians to back your desire to give less.

For my part, I'd rather err on the side of bringing all my tithes into the storehouse. If I'm wrong, what will I lose? Oh, but how much I will gain if I'm right! Here's my benchmark: "Give, and it will be given to you. A good measure, pressed down, shaken together and running over, will be poured into your lap. For with the measure you use, it will be measured to you" (Luke 6:38).

I don't think God will be displeased with me for giving more than he would expect. But if you don't tithe, ask yourself this: "If I want to prosper, can I do so by negotiating how much to return to God?" If you feel guilty about not tithing, that comes from the inside. That's the Holy Spirit convicting you. You just have to listen.

In the New King James Version of Malachi 3:10, it says tithe and "the windows of heaven" will be opened. Not the doors, but the windows. How many windows do you have in your house? Can you even quickly count them? Just imagine — the blessings are so plentiful that they can't fit through the doors. The windows have to be opened so they can pour out!

And let's not forget that God wants us to give above and beyond the tithe: "Whoever sows sparingly will also reap sparingly, and whoever sows generously will also reap generously. Each of you should give what you have decided in your heart to give, not reluctantly or under compulsion, for God loves a cheerful giver" (2 Cor. 9:6–7).

The apostle Paul is right. You are free to give whatever you want. I just encourage you to consider whether or not your giving is what it should be.

> *I never would have been able to tithe the first million dollars I ever made if I had not tithed my first salary, which was $1.50 per week.*
>
> John D. Rockefeller Sr.

TEN TITHING QUESTIONS

I always get a lot of questions about tithing. It doesn't surprise me that it's a hot topic! Based on the questions I get, I've put together a top-ten list of frequently asked questions. I've developed the responses in consultation with my pastor and several other church leaders.

1. *Should I tithe on my gross income (the amount I wish I could bring home) or my net income (the pitiful amount I get to take home after taxes)?*

   As the expression goes, "Do you want a net blessing or a gross blessing?" Seriously, Scripture says to tithe on your "first fruits." You certainly can negotiate your way out of tithing on your gross, arguing that you don't see the money the government takes out for taxes. But that's such a slippery slope. How about tithing after you pay your health insurance or rent or car insurance or any of the many things you are obligated to pay?

   Don't haggle with God when it comes to tithing. Have faith that if you tithe the full 10 percent of your gross income, the remaining 90 percent will meet your needs and satisfy many of your wants.

I do need to clarify the gross versus net debate when it comes to small business owners and entrepreneurs. Business owners should tithe on their personal gross income, not the business gross receipts or revenue. For example, let's say you have a plumbing business that has revenues of $10,000 a month. As the owner, you pay yourself a salary of $3,000 of that $10,000 you receive from customers. You would tithe on your own pay, the $3,000. (And I certainly hope you are paying yourself a regular salary; otherwise what you have is a hobby, not a business.)

Likewise, let's say you made an investment of $1,000, and when you cashed out, the investment had grown to $1,500. Assuming you've already tithed on the $1,000, you would tithe on the "increase," or return on your investment, which is $500.

One more thing on this issue: As a business owner, you should consider having the business tithe. Determine your profit and pay a tithe on it. This wouldn't really be all that different from the charitable contributions to other not-for-profit endeavors that businesses support all the time. So, using the example above, if your business had revenues of $10,000 a month, you would first deduct your costs of doing business. For example, let's say it cost the plumber $6,000 in overhead expenses (salaries, parts, etc.) to generate $10,000. Deducting the $6,000 in costs means the business increase is $4,000. The business would then tithe on the $4,000, or $400.

2. *If I'm laid off and collecting unemployment, do I tithe based on what I was making before or on my unemployment check?*

You would tithe on your current income, which is your unemployment benefit. If your income is just the unemployment check, you tithe on that, not on what you used to earn.

3. *Should I tithe if I'm unemployed and have no income?*

You tithe on your income. If you don't have any income, then you don't have anything to tithe on. However, you may still be able to give an offering. Pray about your situation and ask God first to help you find employment so that you may give again.

4. *Should I tithe even if I'm deeply in debt?*

Yes. I know many people struggle with this question even though they believe in the biblical requirement to tithe. The tithe is holy and it belongs to God (Lev. 27:30). Did you know that by law you can tithe even if you have filed for bankruptcy?

In a New York court case, a judge ruled that a couple couldn't tithe or donate money to charity based on bankruptcy rules that went into effect in 2005. That decision prompted Senator Orrin G. Hatch and then Senator Barack Obama to propose legislation that would allow individuals in bankruptcy to continue giving to churches and charities.

That legislation passed, and now debtors under bankruptcy protection can tithe. The law now says that money given by a debtor to a charitable organization, including tithes, is not to be included when considering the funds available to be paid to a creditor in bankruptcy. That change in the law is good news for tithers. However, there is another biblical principle to keep in mind if you have filed for bankruptcy: "The wicked borrow and do not repay" (Ps. 37:21a). Just as you are called to render your tithes, so too should you make every reasonable attempt to honor your debts.

Here are a few suggestions to help you cut your expenses so you can tithe:

Reduce your cable TV and cell phone bills. People tell me they can't tithe, and yet they spend upwards of $200 a month for cable and a cell phone. You can't argue that you don't have money for God if you're watching HBO and chatting or texting on your cell with your friends.

Get a second job. Look, tithing doesn't make you broke. Living above your means (and spending your tithe) makes you broke. I have never met someone in financial trouble who is down and out solely because he or she tithed.

Connect with a nonprofit organization or a church that can assist with food, clothing, etc. If you are struggling financially, there are resources to help you. Don't be too proud to seek help, which could prevent you from tapping into your tithe to pay your expenses.

5. *I know we are required to render our tithes, but should I also give an offering if I am in debt?*

Yes, the Bible calls for us to give "tithes and offerings." Here are some scriptural guidelines:

> "Then they faithfully brought in the offerings, the tithes, and the dedicated things" (2 Chron. 31:12 NKJV).

> "Will a mere mortal rob God? Yet you rob me. But you ask, 'How are we robbing you?' In tithes and offerings" (Mal. 3:8).

> "But this I say: He who sows sparingly will also reap sparingly, and he who sows bountifully will also reap bountifully. So let each one give as he purposes in his heart, not grudgingly or of necessity; for God loves a cheerful giver. And God is able to make all grace abound toward you, that you, always having all sufficiency in all things, may have an abundance for every good work" (2 Cor. 9:6 – 8 NKJV).

In other words, the tithe is our obligation, but Scripture also says to give above the tithe as the Holy Spirit moves us.

6. *Can I tithe on my time instead of my money?*

No. I look at it this way: Your tithe is used to help fund the administration, facility upkeep, and good works of your local church. Can your church pay the electric bill with your time? No. Tithing means giving money. And you should tithe at the church where you are being spiritually fed on a regular basis — your home church. That doesn't mean you shouldn't also give of your time, but *time don't pay the bills.*

7. *Should I still give if my spouse doesn't believe in tithing?*

This is a tough question and the source of a lot of acrimony in many relationships. I've come across spouses who berate their wives or husbands for not tithing. One wife even told her husband he was damning them to hell for not tithing. Do you think such belligerent behavior is going to win over your spouse and make him or her tithe? It didn't in this woman's case. It hardened her husband's heart toward tithing.

If this issue is creating tension in your household, then you probably have some issues you need to deal with that go beyond tithing.

Please consult your pastor or minister on this issue. But also consider this: If your husband wants you both to tithe, you should follow his lead and "submit" to his leadership. I know. You may have a problem with that word *submit*. But Scripture clearly says, "Wives, submit yourselves to your husbands, as is fitting in the Lord" (Col. 3:18). Ephesians 5:22 – 24 says, "Wives, submit yourselves to your own husbands as you do to the Lord. For the husband is the head of the wife as Christ is the head of the church, his body, of which he is the Savior. Now as the church submits to Christ, so also wives should submit to their husbands in everything."

Trust your husband in this area.

Now what if it's the wife who wants to tithe and her husband is adamantly against it? Ephesians 5:33 says, "The wife must respect her husband." Make an appeal for tithing without becoming disrespectful or belligerent. Do what you can to make your case but don't go against his wishes. You could tithe off the amount of money allocated in your budget for your own personal use. I believe God will honor what you are giving in this situation. Or see if you can get your husband to agree to tithe for a certain period. If he won't agree to that, try this. For a few months, keep track of any unanticipated expenses or bills. Compare the expenses to see if they don't add up to or come close to the amount you would have tithed. Malachi 3:10 says, " 'Test me in this,' says the Lord Almighty, 'and see if I will not throw open the floodgates of heaven and pour out so much blessing that there will not be room enough to store it.' "

If this is an area where there is acrimony, please seek biblically based marital counseling so that you can operate your finances in a godly way. God loves unity.

8. *Should I tithe on a life insurance settlement or an inheritance?*
Yes, you should tithe on this because it is income.

9. *Should I tithe on my social security or pension payments?*

In theory, if all your working life you tithe on your gross income, then when you get your social security or pension benefit, you are just getting back money you put in. Therefore, you would have already tithed on this money. You could calculate the point at which you are no longer getting back your own money from social security and tithe on those funds. However, many people collecting social security benefits will receive far more in benefits than they contributed during their working years. And throughout their working life they didn't tithe. Therefore, the issue is moot; they should tithe.

But let's say you have been a lifelong tither. You could do the math and wait to tithe when you are receiving more than you put in. In this case, let the Holy Spirit lead you in what is the right thing to do.

10. *I get paid once a month. Should I wait until I get paid to tithe or should I just write the check and pray that it doesn't bounce?*

Just as with the rest of your financial life, when you give, you have to act responsibly. It makes no sense to write a check to your church that may be returned for insufficient funds (costing you, and possibly the church too, $35 in bounced check fees). Before you write a check, make sure the funds are available for withdrawal. Pay your tithes when you get your paycheck.

If you want to give your tithe when you worship every Sunday, then you have to plan accordingly. Budget so that you can give your tithe every week without overdrawing your account.

Certainly you may have more questions about tithing than I can answer in this book, so seek the guidance of your minister or pastor. But also go to the Word. Listen to the Holy Spirit. Most importantly, don't let the fear of not having enough rob you of the blessings God has in store for you when you tithe.

TESTIMONY TIME: *Day 4*

When we started paying attention to our finances, my husband and I were approximately $130,000 in debt and had no savings. Since then, we have reduced our debt to $40,000, and have been able to save close to $25,000. Throughout all of this we have continued to tithe and have been amazed at how much we have been able to give.

Kim

TITHING IS NOT A MONEY-BACK GUARANTEE

When you give, God promises you will receive: "'Bring the whole tithe into the storehouse, that there may be food in my house. Test me in this,' says the LORD Almighty, 'and see if I will not throw open the floodgates of heaven and pour out so much blessing that there will not be room enough to store it'" (Mal. 3:10). However, don't misinterpret this Scripture. There's no tit-for-tat with tithing as some people may believe. For them, tithing is seen as a guarantee of a reward. It's not. You should not expect that if you give, you'll get back what you put in and then some.

God isn't a Las Vegas slot machine where you put in coins hoping to hit the jackpot. Rather, he wants us to give as a show of faith that he will reward us in his own time and in his own way with more than what money can buy.

Tithing, above all, is an act of faith.

TESTIMONY TIME: *Day 4*

I have always been a tither, but I tithed off the net, not the gross. After working through my budget, I felt God challenging me to do more. Although I didn't understand how it would work out, I followed the prompting of the Holy Spirit.

God met me where I was and honored that act of obedience:

My employer informed me that I had been underpaid and issued me a check for the difference.

My employer issued me another check because they had underbudgeted for my travel expenses and needed to reimburse me.

My dad wrote me a letter (which was a gift in itself) and I opened it to find a check inside.

I was so encouraged by all of this! And God used these experiences to help me trust him to do even more with my tithing. I called one of my creditors to renegotiate my bills, and I found out that I will have $40 of savings each month. This is just the amount I need to fully tithe on my gross! These principles really work.

Desiree

DAILY ASSIGNMENT

If you are not a tither, make a list of the reasons why you don't tithe. Your list might include things like:

> *I can't afford to tithe.*
> *I am afraid I won't have enough to pay my bills.*

Add up all the nonessential expenses you had in the last month, such as cable, eating out, going to the movies, etc. How much are you spending on these?

Figure out how much your tithes would be per month and compare this with the money you spent on nonessentials. Do you see places you can cut your expenses to find the money to tithe?

If you are already tithing, are you tithing on your gross income? If not, take a look at your discretionary spending (cable, cell phone, entertainment) and consider cutting back so that you can tithe on the full amount of your "increase."

If you already tithe on your gross income, examine your offerings or charitable contributions to other organizations. Are you giving as much as you can? Or are you tithing to the penny, while grousing that you can't or won't give another dime to anything else?

Part Two

FASTING FOR A BETTER FINANCIAL LIFE

Imagine that you are about to take a road trip to an unfamiliar city across the country. I hope one of the first things you would do is map out your trip. Without a map you would probably get off at the wrong interstate exit or end up on the wrong streets and waste time, money, and gas. That's what it's like when you don't prepare yourself to prosper. It's like taking a trip without a map.

The seven chapters in part 2 are your roadmap to prosperity. On our trip, we'll visit the evils of entitlement, the basics of budgeting, and the benefits of saving. We'll also explore the importance of diversifying investments, issues around marriage and money, and the financial legacy we should all be leaving to our children. And don't skip the chapters about marriage and children even if you are single or childless. Your life could change, or you may be able to use what you learn to help someone else.

What ties these chapters together is action. You have to decide to prosper and then go about making that happen. As with a road trip, you won't get to where you are going just sitting in the driveway complaining about all the traffic you will encounter. And you'll increase your chances of getting into a wreck if you don't drive responsibly. Similarly, if you want to prosper, you have to put yourself on the right path and handle your money responsibly.

The Evils of Entitlement

17 Days to Go: The World Is Enticing

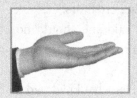

Main Point: A sense of entitlement could be getting in the way of God blessing you.

My Pledge: Today, I'll think about something in my life that I did or purchased that I now realize was giving in to a sense of entitlement.

During the ministry meetings for Prosperity Partners, I often ask members to share their testimony. It takes some prodding, but people eventually open up about what they've learned from participating in the financial fast.

In one particular meeting, Kiesha shot straight up when I asked for volunteers to share how the fast and the ministry had changed their lives.

"I was so excited and wanted to share my testimony," Kiesha recalls. "I proceeded to tell how I had cut back on spending. I felt liberated and was able to save up cash to pay for a trip for me and my mom to go to the Bahamas for Mother's Day that year. I don't know what made Michelle ask me if I had credit card debt, but she did. I admitted that I did. She asked how much. I owed about $8,000. Then she asked how much my trip cost. It was about $2,500. She told me point-blank that I couldn't afford to go on my trip and that I should have used that money to pay down my debt. Needless to say, she burst my bubble, and I was not happy to hear her views."

Kiesha is being kind in recounting that incident. As I was asking her those questions, the people in the room looked at me as if I were body slamming the woman. After all, she had been faithful about adhering to the financial fast. She had drastically cut her spending. She had saved for this wonderful trip to treat her mother. They thought I was being too harsh.

But I stood fast. The fact is, Kiesha was not entitled to that trip. She didn't deserve that trip — not yet. She was not in a position to pay for her mother to go on that trip. She had $8,000 in credit card debt. That $2,500 should have been used to pay off her creditors.

Initially, Kiesha looked wounded when I said she should not have gone on vacation. She stood there for a moment, not sure if she should argue with me.

The room was quiet. I was quiet too, while I let what I had said to Kiesha not just sink in with her but resonate with others in the room. I believe it was the Holy Spirit who pushed me to ask her about her debt. I had no clue about her finances.

Kiesha thought about what I said, and in the first step toward realizing her mistake, she conceded that she should have used her vacation funds to pay down her debt. Her story illustrates that just because you save up for something doesn't mean you get a pat on the back, if you still have debts to pay.

TESTIMONY TIME: *Day 5*

Michelle was right, as always. Although my attitude had taken a move in the right direction, my priorities were not in the right place. I did take my trip since it was paid for and non-refundable, but I took only cash with me for spending money. Sometimes tough love and no-nonsense straight talk from a person without an ulterior motive is what we all need. It's what I needed. The hardest thing was to admit that I had entitlement issues.

Kiesha

THE WORLD IS ENTICING

It's not completely your fault that every day you're tempted to treat yourself to whatever you want, regardless of whether you have the cash to pay for it. We are bombarded with advertising messages that encourage us to give in to our sense of entitlement. The world is really enticing. To feel entitled is to believe you deserve something, such as a certain home or car or lifestyle. It's exactly what Solomon meant when he said, "I denied myself nothing my eyes desired; I refused my heart no pleasure. My heart took delight in all my labor, and this was the reward for all my toil" (Eccl. 2:10). Notice the last line with its emphasis on his toil. Have you ever said you deserve something because of your hard work?

Each day of this fast we're tackling the issues that keep us down financially. One of the biggest issues is a sense of entitlement. How much of the debt people accumulate can be directly related to their sense of entitlement? Too much!

A deep sense of entitlement ruins the opportunity for many of us to be prosperous. Here's just a sample of what many people feel they are entitled to have:

- Vacation
- Luxury car
- House
- Designer clothes
- The "perfect" wedding
- Ivy League education
- Dining out
- Entertainment
- Latest electronic gadgets

So do you or have you felt entitled to anything on this list? Have any of these items caused you to go into debt or delay getting out of debt? This is an important issue you have to address. What are you chasing after? Solomon realized his mistake. He wrote, "Yet when I surveyed all that my hands had done and what I had toiled to achieve, everything was meaningless, a chasing after the wind; nothing was gained under the sun" (Eccl. 2:11). I love the imagery in that verse. We chase things and wealth, but to what avail? Just like you can't capture wind in your hand, you can't gain God's favor by pursuing material things you feel you're entitled to.

And still we chase, all the while telling ourselves that we deserve it. In fact, here are some of the things people say to convince themselves that they are entitled to certain things:

"I work hard."

"I didn't have a lot as a child."

"You can't take it with you!"

"I can afford it."

"I can put it on my credit card."

"It's on sale."

"Everybody has one."

"I deserve the best."

"If I'm going to be in debt, I might as well have what I want."

"What will people say if I don't wear the right clothes, drive a nice car, or send my children to the best schools?"

"If my neighbors can have it, I can too."

"I want my children to have it better than I did."

"God wants me to be happy."

You need to be mindful of your internal dialogue about your desires. If you are not careful, the evil of entitlement will put you in financial jeopardy.

I understand that you want so much for your life. I get that you may have felt deprived as a child. Or perhaps you were spoiled as a child, and you've carried that sense of entitlement into adulthood. It's hard to shake these feelings, especially when it appears everyone else around you is getting what they want. I realize that you work hard. Still, you aren't entitled to what you want until you can truly afford it.

You have to get rid of your entitlement issues, and the financial fast is a great way to start.

Looking back on your life, can you identify a time when a sense of entitlement may have sabotaged your finances? Has pride ever driven you to purchase something you didn't need and couldn't afford? Have you tried to convince yourself that luxurious "wants" are really "needs" in order to justify spending money you didn't have? In your journaling for today, really contemplate these questions. I'm serious. If you're determined to get your financial life together, take the time.

Even if you are a faithful steward, complete the task. I've done this myself. Although my hobby is saving money, there are times when I, too, give in to entitlement. For example, for the longest time I refused to give in to my husband's pleas to turn the heat down in our home. I hate to be cold. So most of the time our house felt like a hot day in the Caribbean. Since I was frugal in so many other ways, I felt I deserved to have some heat in the house, no matter the cost. My husband totaled the heating bills for the year and showed me how much we were spending to keep me feeling like I was in Jamaica (not to mention how much energy we were using). I was finally convicted in this area. So now we have a programmable thermostat to moderate the temperature in our house, and I wear heavy sweatpants and shirts and socks to bed, even in the summer (that's the price my husband has to pay).

I'm certainly not saying you shouldn't want nice things for yourself, but at what cost? When do the "wants" end? I've seen the ramifications of people getting what they say they deserve. They end up in homes that are beautiful, but they have to work long hours away from home to pay the mortgage. They buy cars with monthly payments that are more like mortgages. I worked with an individual whose car payments exceeded $1,000 a month — for one vehicle. People with a sense of entitlement take great vacations only to come back to voice-mail messages from creditors trying to hunt them down. For those whose entitlement issues are clothes or shoes, they look nice, but their bank accounts are in tatters.

And we are passing this sense of entitlement on to our children.

I wish I could open up the heads of some parents and drop a little bit of my grandmother's common sense into their brains. I once visited a high school to talk to a class of teens about money management. Right in the middle of my presentation, a kid jumped up and left the room when his cell phone rang.

"Wait," I said as he headed out the door. "Who is that on the telephone and why is he or she calling you while you're in class?"

"It's my mother," the student snapped. "I have a doctor's appointment and she's calling to remind me."

Mind you, he didn't need to leave for the appointment right then. I blame that boy's mama for his rude behavior. All she needed to do was send a note with him to school telling him what time she was going to pick him up. If he wasn't outside when she got there, she could go into the school and have him called to the office.

That episode got me wondering why so many parents have bought into this idea that their children need cell phones, which are now as prevalent among preteens and teens as acne.

And don't give me that baloney that it was purchased for just emergency use. It's because the kid felt entitled to the phone. It is even more likely that the teen or preteen — egged on by masterful marketing and peer pressure — whined for a cell phone and some adult just caved. The reality is that cell phones are used the majority of the time by non-business consumers for idle chatter or texting. Is your kid texting and talking away money that could be used for a college fund?

> *A man is rich in proportion to the number of things which he can afford to let alone.*
>
> Henry David Thoreau

The world doesn't just *seem* enticing. It *is* enticing. Throughout your life you will be tempted to give in to your sense of entitlement. But you must exercise some self-control. The things you seek to satisfy whatever is missing in your life are temporary. If you truly want to use your money to reflect your values, you need to get rid of any entitlement issues. In the next section I'll show you how to do that.

ATTITUDE OF GRATITUDE

One of the surest ways to combat the evils of entitlement is to develop a grateful attitude. We want so much for ourselves and our families that we often don't stop to look at what we already have.

When I was younger, I complained to my grandmother, Big Mama, that the other children had better clothes or shoes than I did. I complained that they got to eat out or go to the movies. Wasn't I entitled to have some of those things? After all, I pointed out to her, I was a good student. I did my chores.

Big Mama, being the pragmatic person she was, pointed out that I should be grateful for a roof over my head and that I had clothes at all. I could go to the refrigerator and get some food or walk over to the sink and get a clean glass of water. Most importantly, she pointed out, I might have ended up in foster care with much less. It was a harsh way to respond to my griping — that I should be grateful that I wasn't thrown into the foster-care system — but I understand now what she was doing. She was telling me I may not be where I want to be, but I should be glad I didn't end up in a worse situation.

So I learned to count my blessings. I had to wear "fish head" sneakers, as the children called the off-brand shoes my grandmother purchased for me and my siblings. With five grandchildren to take care of, she couldn't afford to buy the "cooler" Jack Purcell sneakers that the kids were wearing in Baltimore at the time. Nonetheless, my feet were covered, and I could run and jump like the rest of the children. I learned from my fish-head sneaker days that to increase my wealth I had to decrease my wants. And guess what? It works.

If you want to graduate from a sense of entitlement to contentment, try this:

- Exercise self-control. Wait thirty days before you buy something.
  Chances are you won't want the item once you've spent some time
  thinking about it.

- Establish financial priorities. When you stay focused on getting the
  things you say you really value, you won't waste your money.

- Calculate how long you have to work to get the things you feel you're
  entitled to. On *www.MoreBusiness.com* you will find a "Time Is
  Money" calculator designed to help you decide if your purchases
  are really worth your time and money. (The direct link is *http://
  www.morebusiness.com/time-is-money-calculator.*) The calculator
  automatically estimates your federal tax bracket (and an average
  state income tax bracket) to come up with the total number of hours
  you need to work to buy something. For example, let's say you earn
  $40,000 a year, and you feel you've worked hard and deserve a $2,000
  big-screen television. You would have to work 155 hours to pay for
  that TV, or nineteen days if you work a normal eight-hour shift.

- Curtail your television viewing. Advertising feeds right into a sense
  of entitlement. If you have TiVo or a digital video recorder (DVR),
  just zoom through the commercials. You can't want what you don't
  see. In fact, there's a rule in my house to help my children avoid nag-
  ging me for things they see on television. The rule is they can't get
  anything they first see on a television commercial. I always tell this
  joke that my daughter, Jillian, ran into the kitchen panting and asking me to buy her some toy. I asked her where she learned about the
  toy. She knew she was trapped. She thought for a second and said, "It
  came to me in a dream."

- Don't use shopping as a form of entertainment. Even after the fast,
  treat shopping outings like a chore. If you have entitlement issues,
  going to the mall is like an alcoholic hanging out at a bar. Why
  tempt yourself?

How much richer could you be if you eliminated the things you think you're entitled to? I understand that if you've had a rough childhood, marriage, or work life, you may feel you need to do things or buy things to make yourself feel better. But I know where you can find fulfillment that won't cost you a dime. Try God. Try leaning on him for relief and watch the rewards you will receive. God knows your desires, so give him a chance to bring peace into your life. Get rid of your sense of entitlement, and you may find a much better life with riches untold.

DAILY ASSIGNMENT

Think of an occasion where you gave in to your sense of entitlement. For example, did you take a vacation that ended up putting you further into debt?

How much did your sense of entitlement cost you? Write down the amount so you can own up to it.

Today I want you to list at least three things you are grateful for. Then, in a specific prayer, I want you to give thanks to God for those blessings. As the song goes, "Count your blessings, name them one by one." The following are examples of things to be grateful for:

- *I have a job.*
- *I have someplace to live.*
- *I have my own teeth.*

You Can't Buy Contentment

16 Days to Go: Satisfaction Guaranteed

Main Point: Be content with what you have.

My Pledge: Today, I promise I will not complain about anything I don't have.

I recall one birthday where I was so happy. I smiled so much people kept asking me why I was so blissful.

It wasn't because I had received flowers for my birthday. I don't really like cut flowers because they die, and I just think that's a waste of money.

It wasn't because my husband was going to take me someplace special for dinner. He wasn't. I was cooking dinner. He hadn't bought me a card because I told him he could save the five dollars and just tell me he loves me. Ditto on a gift.

Finally I figured out what was making me so happy. I was content.

I did a mental inventory of my life, and I was just tickled at what God had done for me. I have a great husband who, although he doesn't give me as many foot massages as I'd like, is a wonderful provider, lover, friend, and father. He really does have the patience of Job, which he needs to live with me.

Even though my three children can get on my last nerve, they're good kids. They do well in school. Most important, they are kind, loving, and funny. I appreciate that my oldest child is still alive. When she was seven, she nearly died from a rare blood condition. At the start of her teen years, I told

To be content is to be happy.

Chinese proverb

her God spared her life so I could kill her. (If you're a parent with a teenager, I'm sure you understand.) Still I'm grateful for the mother-daughter spats. After all, she's alive.

I have good friends. A good job (heck, depending on the current state of the economy, any job is a good job). I have my health, my eyesight, and my own teeth. I can walk over to the sink and get a clean glass of water. My cupboards aren't bare, as evidenced by my spreading hips. I have heat, even though my husband won't let me turn it up much. I'm a homeowner. I finally learned to ride a bike even though I was well into my thirties when I did.

I was happy on that birthday because I didn't want for much.

TESTIMONY TIME: *Day 6*

I learned during the fast that you don't have to always spend, spend, and spend to enjoy what life has to offer. I now enjoy spending time with my family at home instead of going to a crowded restaurant where there are so many distractions. I learned that I don't require as much as I once thought I did. It's all just stuff, and my husband (bless his heart) was always trying to please me with the stuff that I wanted. I realize how much pressure I was putting on him to make sure he made enough money to provide these things for me.

The fast helped me examine why I felt I expected all these things from my husband. It all goes back to my childhood and how my father, who was not around much, would shower me with expensive gifts. I grew up thinking that this is what a man does for you to show his love. I now understand that it was my father's guilt of not spending time with me that made him shower me with gifts. So when I got married, I put those expectations on my husband.

I am a changed person now. Most importantly, I have peace of mind knowing that I don't need to have stuff to have a happy life.

Trina

CONTENTMENT ISN'T FOR SALE

Are you content?

I find I have to ask that question, because clearly many folks aren't. I know this because of all the stuff folks keep buying, trying to gain that contentment.

If you've stuck strictly to the fast so far, you may be feeling a little low because you haven't been shopping or eating out or entertaining yourself the way you used to. You may be feeling a lack of contentment. A lack of contentment is a little different than having a sense of entitlement, which we addressed on Day 5. Having a sense of entitlement means you feel you deserve something you don't have. Lack of contentment means you aren't satisfied with what you *do* have.

The marketing folks at Toyota created a great illustration of discontentment in a series of commercials for their "Toyotathon Phenomenon" sales promotions. In the ads, people wreck absolutely good cars and trucks so they can justify buying new Toyota vehicles. In one commercial, a dapperly dressed businessman, briefcase in hand, stands next to his truck on the rooftop of a parking garage. He sets down his briefcase and pushes his truck over the edge of the facility. He watches as it plunges to the ground and is totaled. Now, having destroyed a perfectly fine truck, he can get the new Toyota he always "wanted." In another commercial, a man rushes to bury his Corolla sedan under mounds of snow so that an approaching snow plow will demolish it as it rolls by.

I've actually had vehicles that looked like they should be pushed off the top of a parking garage. The bumpers were missing. There were so many dings and dents it was hard to tell where they stopped. But the truck and car the men in the Toyota ads were destroying were in good shape, nary a ding or dent in sight. Near the end of one of the commercials an announcer says, "There's never been a better time to get the new truck you always *wanted* or needed."

There it is.

The advertisers know our weakness. We don't wait for our needs to be met; we spend or go into debt for our wants. That's a lack of contentment.

I have a quick remedy for the lack of contentment. Clean your house.

Clean every room. Start with your child's bedroom and then move to the playroom, family room, or wherever you store their playthings. Dump out the toy bins and boxes. Pull out *all* the books, every toy, game, electronic game system (or systems), and the software and accessories. Next, go to your own room. Clean your bedroom closet. Then go down the hall and clean out the closet you use in the spare bedroom. Go through the cabinets and drawers in your kitchen. Clean the basement. Clean the garage, if you have one. Go visit the storage space you're renting. Just open the door and look at all the stuff you've accumulated over the years.

I dare you.

Take out everything and just stand there and look at it all. Make a list of it and then tell me why you don't feel content. If we equate having stuff with contentment, then why aren't we satisfied considering all the stuff we have?

Does this sound like something you've said:

"They have a better car than we have."

"If I had their money, I would be so happy."

"Our house isn't as nice as theirs. We need to move."

We feed into our lack of contentment by complaining. And we complain because we're coveting what others have.

The apostle Paul talks about what it means to be content: "I know what it is to be in need, and I know what it is to have plenty. I have learned the secret of being content in any and every situation, whether well fed or hungry, whether living in plenty or in want" (Phil. 4:12). If you've grown up in a church, you've heard this Scripture plenty of times. The question is, do you believe you can find that safety zone of contentment Paul found? Can you learn the secret of contentment whether you are in need or have plenty?

This is what I've come to realize about people who are in need:

- They often lose faith in God.
- They think their finances will never be right.
- They think if they just earned more money they would be happy.
- They become desperate, resorting to payday loans or living off credit cards.

This is what I've come to realize about people who have plenty:

- They continually want more.
- They fail to save the extra money they have for times when they may be in need.
- They spoil themselves.
- They spoil their children.
- They forget to thank God.

Here's what both groups have in common: Those who are without aren't content and those who have a lot aren't content. When people say, "If only I were rich," I ask them what would be different. My experience has been that the only difference when you're rich is that your problems are more expensive. If all it took was money to be happy, then rich people wouldn't have "issues." And we know they do; the tabloids tell us so.

So, can you see the foolishness of being discontent? It's an equal-opportunity sin — it doesn't care whether you're destitute or filthy rich. It wreaks havoc on your life no matter what your circumstances may be.

When the apostle Paul describes the secret of contentment, he is describing a state of equilibrium in which we don't whine when we are in want and we don't take pride in our prosperity.

When you are in need, you have to believe God will provide. When you are prosperous, you have to learn not to be so overconfident that you overspend. The latter is perhaps the harder lesson because the temptation is so great. Intellectually and spiritually we know contentment can't be measured by the amount of money or possessions we have, and yet practically we act as if it does.

TESTIMONY TIME: *Day 6*

Before the fast, I was living from paycheck to paycheck, hoping that the next promotion and raise was on its way. I had to learn how to be content in limiting the amount of food I purchased, the places I visited (to save on gas), and the purchases I made. Reality has set in, and now I am seeking the Lord about a roommate or even selling my house so that I can live according to God's Word. This requires me to be content because I can no longer afford to be foolish in the handling of my finances. Even my relatives are changing their spending habits as I explain to them the necessary changes I have made.

Deborah

DAILY ASSIGNMENT

Make a list of at least three things you've said lately that express a lack of contentment. For example:

- *I wish I had a bigger house.*
- *I don't have anything to wear.*
- *We never go anywhere.*

After you make the list, ask God for forgiveness for not appreciating what you have.

Clean out your house. You didn't think I was kidding, did you? Well, maybe not the whole house today. Instead, pick one room or a closet or toy bin and pull everything out. Sort everything into three piles: keep it, trash it, give it away. Give or throw away everything you haven't used in the last year.

The Benefits of Budgeting

15 Days to Go: Budgeting for Life

Main Point: A budget is your roadmap to prosperity.

My Pledge: I will be diligent and develop a budget so that every penny I earn has a purpose.

Today the hard work begins. Yup, you have to do a budget. If you have a budget already, that's wonderful, but is it written down either on paper or on your computer?

Lots of people are intimidated by budgeting. Or they think it restricts what they can do. In its annual Economy and Personal Finance survey, Gallup asked Americans about the financial tools they used. Few Americans (30 percent) prepare a long-term financial plan outlining their savings and investment goals in detail. Only one in three prepare a budget.

Before you start your budget, you need to realize that budgeting isn't about you. It's about good stewardship and managing the resources God has given to you. Budget well and tithing is not a problem. Budget well and you can save for a home, a car, a college education, and retirement. Budget well and you bring order to your financial life. The psalmist writes, "The Lord makes firm the steps of the one who delights in him" (Ps. 37:23).

What happens when you don't budget? You find yourself saying things like:

"I don't know where all my money goes."

"I just got $60 out of the ATM, and I don't know what I spent it on."

"I don't know how that check bounced."

"I get paid and I'm broke before the week is out."

"I can never seem to get ahead."

"I keep raiding my rainy-day fund."

"I hate payday."

I actually heard that last statement from a young father. With watery eyes he said he hated payday because before he even cashed his check, it was all spent on bills. You can't keep living without a plan for your money. That's like going on a cross-country trip to visit cities and towns you've never been to before, only you don't have a roadmap. No map, you get lost. It's the same with your finances. No budget, you get lost.

TEN BENEFITS OF BUDGETING

I know you won't follow through and set up a budget unless you see the benefit. So let me ask you this question: How's *not* having a budget working for you? It's probably not. If I told you that budgeting would lead to financial peace, would you create one for yourself?

Diligence is the basis of wealth.

Chinese proverb

Well, I'm telling you budgeting will bring order, and order brings peace. It won't be easy to sit down and do your budget. It's a scary thing to face what you already know — that you don't have enough income to cover your expenses. But not knowing is worse. And it's worse because ignoring your financial situation will keep you stressed out. In the end, preparing a budget will:

1. Help you to spend your money on the things that really matter to you.

2. Help put you in control of your money so your money doesn't control you.

3. Help tell you if you're living within your means.

4. Help you meet your savings goals.

5. Help your entire family focus on common goals.

6. Help you prepare for emergencies.

7. Help you manage variable expenses, such as car insurance payments.

8. Help reveal areas where you're spending too much.

9. Help keep you out of debt or help get you out of debt.

10. Help you sleep better at night.

That's a pretty good list of benefits, don't you think? It will help if you keep these things in mind while you're doing the hard work of budgeting. It's a tedious process that can reveal to you those areas where you spend that you would rather keep hidden. During one ministry meeting I asked those members who had not prepared a budget to speak up. Several people sheepishly raised their hands. One woman in particular confessed that despite my pleading, and that of her mentor, she still couldn't face doing a budget.

"What's keeping you from doing a budget?" I asked.

"I just don't know," she said.

"Oh, come on, be honest with yourself," I persisted. "Why can't you face doing a budget?"

Finally, with tears welling up in her eyes, she confessed. "I'm in my fifties, and I can't believe I let my finances get like this," she said. "I'm embarrassed, and a budget will only show me how bad things are."

That woman's honesty was a revelation for others who hadn't admitted that they too hadn't done their budgets. As I told her, though, as bad as things looked without a budget, not having one was worse. Complete a budget, and things can only get better.

The benefits of budgeting tremendously outweigh the dreary job of preparing one. If nothing else, you become aware of what needs fixing, and with that knowledge you can begin a plan to improve your financial situation.

TESTIMONY TIME: *Day 7*

As an accountant, you would think I know better about some things, but bad habits die hard. I come from a family that often made bad financial decisions, and I have to continually resist unwise financial choices.

I had a budget before the fast, but I'm using it much more faithfully now. I'm not 100 percent yet, but I'm getting there. And my credit score has improved—it's gone up more than ninety points in less than two years!

Alison

INSTRUCTIONS FOR BUILDING YOUR BUDGET

Read these instructions completely before developing your budget plan. At the end of these instructions, you'll find a sample budget template. You can use the blank forms in the Appendix or download the template in an Excel format from *www.michellesingletary.com*. Enter your budget amounts into the white spaces in the Excel template, and the template will calculate your totals for you in the shaded spaces. Not familiar with Excel? Download the printable version of the template and enter your figures with a pencil. (You'll have to calculate the totals yourself, though.)

Don't be intimidated by the length of the budget and all the expense line items. The budget template is detailed because I want you to try to account for every penny you make and spend. Plus, you'll likely find that a number of expenses won't even apply to you. Just leave those lines blank. And no matter how often your employer pays you — every week, every two weeks, once or twice per month — this budget template will work for you.

Going through this budget exercise just once will be a real eye opener for you. It will show you things about how you spend your money that may surprise you! So don't delay. If you put it off, you could be putting off the prosperity God has in store for you.

Okay, let's get started!

INSTRUCTIONS FOR THE BUDGET TEMPLATE

The budget template has two worksheets: Income and Expenses. In the Excel version, you can move back and forth between the worksheets by clicking on the tabs at the bottom left-hand side of your screen. On the Income worksheet, simply input all the money you earn from all sources. The Total Gross Income is the sum of all your sources of income.

Next, enter your Net Income (take-home pay) in the space provided. You can take this figure straight from your paycheck (or pay stub if your pay is deposited directly to your bank account).

On the Expenses worksheet, you'll see that both the Total Gross Income and the Net Income figures have carried over from the Income worksheet. Your job is to fill in the rest of the figures to complete your budget. Here are some other terms you will see in the Expenses worksheet:

Tithing: Many budgets include this line item near the bottom of the budget. But here, it's at the top — where it should be. Giving, especially paying tithes, should be a priority in your budget. The template automatically calculates a 10 percent tithe on your gross income. If you don't tithe, you can delete the inserted figure and leave that space blank.

Net Spendable Income: This is the amount (after taxes, tithes, and payroll deductions) that you have to cover your expenses. Again, if you don't tithe, the net spendable income is what you bring home minus deductions.

Monthly Expenses: This is the total of all the numbers you are about to enter in the spaces below. It will add up automatically. (You don't need to worry about that for now.)

Difference: This will show you how much extra money you have after the expenses are paid. If it's a positive number, that's good. On the other hand, if it's a negative number, meaning you have more bills than money, please don't panic! This is very important information you can now use to start making some changes in how you spend your resources. But before you get to that positive or negative number, you've got some work to do.

The Expenses worksheet has columns labeled as follows: Monthly Expenses Paid from Each Paycheck, Pay Period (1, 2, etc.), Monthly Expenses Total, Target Percentage, and Actual Percentage. Here's what each means:

Monthly Expenses Paid from Each Paycheck: This is the amount you've budgeted for your various expenses out of each paycheck. The fact is, we must pay our expenses based on how much money we earn and how frequently we receive it during the month. Unless you get one paycheck a month, you have to figure out what expenses are paid from which paycheck. So, in these spaces enter the amounts that you receive as often as you receive them.

Pay Period: Many budgets are designed for you to calculate what you spend on a monthly basis. However, I've found that people can't always figure out what expenses should be paid out of which paycheck without some additional planning. Therefore, you can use this template to help figure it out:

- A budget for people who get paid **weekly**. Usually, these people get paid four times per month, but two times each year they will get paid five times. Therefore, there is a fifth column for the months in which you have a fifth paycheck.

- A budget for people who get paid **biweekly**, or who get twenty-six paychecks a year. Similar to those who get paid weekly, you will use a third column for the two months in which you have a third paycheck. This should help you budget better and not see that extra paycheck as money that can be blown.

- A budget for people who get paid **twice a month**, or who get twenty-four paychecks a year. In this case, you would use Pay Periods 1 and 2 for every month.

- A budget for people who get paid **once a month**, or who get twelve paychecks a year. In this case you would use only Pay Period 1.

If you get paid more than once a month, then the pay period columns can help you determine which paycheck you should use to pay certain monthly bills. For example, if your rent or mortgage is due at the beginning of the month, you would take the money for this expense out of your first paycheck of the month (or maybe from the last paycheck of the previous month). Likewise, if your utility bill is due near the end of the month, you would plan to pay that bill with your second paycheck for the month. This should help you ensure that money is available to pay these expenses on time instead of being late because you're waiting for the next paycheck to come.

Monthly Expenses Total: This column totals your monthly expenses for each subcategory (i.e., Savings, Housing, Utilities, etc.).

Target Percentage: People often ask what percentage of their monthly budget they should be spending on housing or food or transportation. The target percentage provides a recommended percentage of your *net spendable income* that should be used for certain categories. The ranges for each target percentage are based on my work with individuals as well as interviews with credit counseling agencies and other financial experts. You will notice only the major expense categories have target percentages.

Actual Percentage: This column will show how your spending compares with the target percentage range. Please keep in mind that the target percentage will vary depending on your family size, where you live, and other factors. But generally, you'll want to stay within this range. Not every expense has a target percentage goal. There's a goal just for the major expense categories.

GET READY, GET SET ...

Now that we've covered how the budget template works, here are some additional guidelines to help you get off to a strong start.

Before you sit down to begin your budget, be sure to collect all relevant documents you'll need to identify the proper amounts for each line item. For the income section, gather earnings statements or pay stubs from each employer, pension/social security/other income statements, and self-employment income such as commissions, invoices, sales records, etc.

For the expenses section, gather all bills or statements for monthly recurring expenses like utilities, rent, insurance, property taxes, phone (landline and cellular), insurance premiums, court orders requiring payments (child support, alimony, etc.), and other out-of-pocket expenses.

For income or expenses that do not occur monthly (such as property taxes that aren't included in your mortgage), you should convert the payment to a monthly amount to be sure you are putting away enough money every month to pay the bill when it comes due. To calculate the monthly amount for property taxes that are billed once a year, divide the total amount owed each year by twelve. Keep this money separate from your regular checking or savings account; otherwise, you may be tempted to spend it.

If you're self-employed, keep in mind you need to put money away for income taxes. Remember, you have to pay both the employee and the employer's share of FICA. However, you are allowed to deduct half of this self-employment tax as a business expense.

I've added a section for bank fees paid to banks, credit cards, etc. You should minimize or eliminate these fees as much as possible, especially fees associated with overdrawing your bank account or paying late on your bills. Your goal should be to pay zero dollars in fees, but the reality is that things happen, and you may well pay these kinds of bank fees, so there's no point in ignoring them. Instead, include them in your budget so you can see how much you're paying. Once you understand how much you're giving away without getting anything in return, you'll surely start to do what's necessary to avoid getting hit with fees in the first place.

It's very important that you pay attention to your budget every month! A budget isn't something you can create, put aside, and then expect to magically help you control your spending.

Now you're ready to build your budget. Once you've completed your budget, look for areas where you are overspending. For example, I was working with a young, single mother, and after going through her budget I saw that she was spending almost $120 a month for cell phone service. I had her call the provider and downgrade to a lower-cost plan for about $60 a month. The new plan meant fewer minutes, of course, and no texting, but she needed that extra $60 to help pay off her debts.

If things aren't adding up, or if you're over in certain budget categories, the table on the opposite page shows some money-saving tips to help you balance your budget.

Once you've captured all the basic information and set an initial budget, the next step is to figure out if your spending is out of whack. Most people can tell you pretty much to the penny how much their mortgage or rent is every month. They can also tell you how much they pay each month for their car loan. But ask them what percentage of their income should be allocated for housing or transportation, and they hesitate. Avoid raiding your rainy-day fund for anything other than truly unexpected emergencies by budgeting for the things that you can plan for. For instance, a vacation is not something that is unexpected. You can plan for it. If you like to have nice and expensive clothes, that's okay. But what's not okay is shopping without a budget

Money-Saving Tips	Monthly Savings
Save 50 cents per day in loose change	$15
Eliminate soda pop consumption	$6
Make your own coffee	$40
Take a brown-bag lunch to work (savings @ $5/day)	$100
Eat out 2 fewer times a month	$50
Subscribe to basic cable only	$50
Reduce cell phone plan minutes	$45
Stop bouncing checks	$35
Pay credit card bill on time	$25
Pay off $1,000 of credit card debt, reducing interest	$15
TOTAL MONTHLY SAVINGS = $381	

limit. Tithing should help you budget better. Giving 10 percent of your gross income puts you in the financial mood to make what's left stretch to cover what else is important in your life.

TESTIMONY TIME: *Day 7*

After recognizing my haphazard spending habits, I realized that to be financially responsible, I had to do some planning. So I started taking my lunch to work every day (which meant I had to plan for this in my grocery shopping). And when I knew I would be gone from home for several hours, I packed a snack to take along so that when I got hungry and was nowhere near the house, I could still eat without spending money.

I identified other areas that weren't truly needs, like my $150 cable bill and the $40 to $80 per week on specialized basketball lessons for my daughter when the Boys and Girls Club cost only $80 for the year.

I signed up for budget billing on my utilities—which stabilized the fluctuation from month to month—and stopped contributing to monthly birthday lunches and gifts for coworkers.

Eliminating the leaks from my budget allowed me to start a savings account and deposit $50 per month. I used this amount to build up my emergency fund and made sure the money was deposited by setting up an automatic transfer from

my checking to my savings each month. That way I couldn't accidentally spend the
money before the end of the month and end up with nothing. This savings account,
along with the reductions in my monthly living expenses, helped me develop disci-
pline and a different mind-set about money.

I learned that I'm not supposed to spend the money until it's gone. I also
learned that I could actually live with a lot less than what I previously thought was
"necessary."

Adrienne

BUDGET BASICS

One important part of budgeting is understanding how your spending compares with your net income (the amount you take home).
What percentage of your net income are you spending on housing?
Do you know what percentage you *should* be spending on a place
to live?

In general, you should not spend more than 36 percent of your
take-home pay on housing. That, of course, is an ideal situation. However, I know that in high-cost-of-living areas, people may spend 40 to
50 percent of their net pay on housing. But when you begin to reach
those percentage levels, it becomes difficult, if not impossible, to save
and invest. If half of your pay is going to this one expense category,
then you have to do something to bring that percentage down — get
a roommate (or roommates), earn extra income, or move. I know, I
know. That's easier said than done. But unless you do something to
keep your spending in various areas in line with certain percentage
ranges, you will always be broke.

The chart on the next page will give you percentage guidelines for
major expense categories. Please note these percentage guidelines are
just that — guidelines. All the percentages are based on your net pay,
meaning what you bring home after taxes. Depending on your situation — where you live and your family size — you may spend more

SUGGESTED PERCENTAGES FOR MAJOR BUDGET ITEMS

Category	Percentage Range
Tithe	10%
Offering/Charitable Giving	2 – 10%
Saving/investing	2 – 10%
Housing (mortgage/rent, insurance, taxes)	26 – 36%
Food (groceries, dining out, workday meals)	12 – 30%
Utilities (gas, electricity, water, cell, landline)	4 – 8%
Transportation (car loan, gas, public transit)	6 – 15%
Medical (dental, prescriptions, health insurance)	4 – 10%
Child care (if applicable)	6 – 16%
Non-mortgage debt obligations (eg.: credit card, personal loans)	5 – 10%
Clothing	4 – 6%
Recreation/entertainment	2 – 8%

or less in certain categories. However, if you find, for example, that you are spending 40 percent of your net pay on housing, you have to cut somewhere else. What's included in your budget and the percentage of your income that you spend in any one expense category will depend on your personal financial situation. If one or more budget items are considerably more than the generally recommended ranges, that means you have to reduce your spending either in that area or elsewhere in your budget.

American humorist Cooley Mason said, "A budget takes the fun out of money." That's an amusing line, but it's only true if you view budgeting as limiting what you can do. I choose to view a budget as liberating. If you commit to budgeting, it will allow you to have fun because you'll be able to plan for the party. Most of all, a budget gives you financial direction. Without it you can become lost. You aren't sure where your money's going, or you aren't using it for what really matters to you. With all due respect to Mr. Mason, there's nothing fun about being lost.

SAMPLE BUDGET WORKSHEET

Note: The dollar amounts listed are only used as an example. The net income figure only represents federal taxes withheld to make the example as simple as possible. Your net pay will of course depend on your own deductions including federal, state, and local taxes.

INCOME

INCOME	Pay Period 1	Pay Period 2	Pay Period 3	Pay Period 4	Pay Period 5	Monthly Totals
Wages/Salary/Tips	$2,500.00	$2,500.00				$5,000.00
Commissions/Bonuses						$
Social Security/Pension/Retirement						$
Alimony						$
Child Support						$
Interest/Dividend Income						$
Disability, VA Benefits						$
Other Income						$
Total Gross Income	$2,500.00	$2,500.00	$	$	$	$5,000.00
Net Income (Take-home pay)	$2,028.70	$2,028.70				$4,057.40

EXPENSES

	Pay Period 1	Pay Period 2	Pay Period 3	Pay Period 4	Pay Period 5	Monthly Totals
Total Gross Income	$2,500.00	$2,500.00	$	$	$	$5,000.00
Net Income (Take-home pay)	$2,028.70	$2,028.70	$	$	$	$4,057.40
Tithes (10% of Gross Income)	$250.00	$250.00	$	$	$	$500.00
Net Spendable Income	$1,778.70	$1,778.70	$	$	$	$3,557.40
Monthly Expenses	$2,680.00	$875.00	$	$	$	$3,555.00
Difference	$(901.30)	$903.70	$	$	$	$2.40

*The information for this top box (Net Spendable Income and Monthly Expenses) is pulled from the information you'll input for your monthly expenses. Negative numbers (in parentheses) mean you are spending more than your net spendable income. If so, then you need to reduce your expenses, increase your income, or both. On the other hand, if you have money left over after paying your expenses, use it to accelerate paying off debts and/or to increase your savings.

	Monthly Expenses Paid from Each Paycheck					Monthly Expense Total	Target Percentage	Actual Percentage
	Pay Period 1	Pay Period 2	Pay Period 3	Pay Period 4	Pay Period 5			
Savings	$125.00	$125.00	$	$	$	$250.00	2-10%	7%
Emergency Savings	$100.00	$100.00				$200.00		
Life Happens Savings Fund	$25.00	$25.00				$50.00		
Retirement Savings						$		
College Savings						$		

Continued on next page

	Monthly Expenses Paid from Each Paycheck					Monthly Expense Total	Target Percentage	Actual Percentage
	Pay Period 1	Pay Period 2	Pay Period 3	Pay Period 4	Pay Period 5			
Housing	$1,200.00	$	$	$	$	$1,200.00	26-36%	34%
Mortgage/Rent	$1,200.00					$1,200.00		
Home Equity Loan or Line of Credit (HELOC)						$		
Property Tax						$		
Home Owners/Condo Association Dues/Fees						$		
Homeowner's/Renter's Insurance						$		
Utilities	$485.00	$	$	$	$	$485.00	4-8%	14%
Electricity	$200.00					$200.00		
Natural Gas/Oil						$		
Water/Sewer						$		
Phone (landline)	$75.00					$75.00		
Cell Phone	$90.00					$90.00		
Cable TV, Internet service	$120.00					$120.00		
Food	$300.00	$300.00	$	$	$	$600.00	12-30%	17%
Groceries	$150.00	$150.00				$300.00		
Meals Out	$100.00	$100.00				$200.00		

Workplace lunch, snacks	$50.00	$50.00				$100.00		
School lunch, snacks						$		
Family Obligations	$		$		$	$	6-16%	0%
Child Support						$		
Alimony						$		
Childcare						$		
Private school tuition						$		
Music/Sports Lessons						$		
Nursing Home/Health Aid/Senior Care						$		
Transportation	$450.00	$100.00	$		$	$550.00	6-15%	15%
Auto Payments	$350.00					$350.00		
Gasoline	$100.00	$100.00				$200.00		
Auto Insurance						$		
Public transportation/parking						$		
Insurance (if not deducted from pay)	$		$		$	$	4%	0%
Medical						$		
Dental/Vision						$		
Life						$		
Disability						$		

	Monthly Expenses Paid from Each Paycheck					Monthly Expense Total	Target Percentage	Actual Percentage
	Pay Period 1	Pay Period 2	Pay Period 3	Pay Period 4	Pay Period 5			
Health Expenses	$	$	$	$	$	$	4%	0%
Medical/dental copays/Expenses						$		
Medications						$		
Medical Supplies						$		
Debt Payments	$120.00	$250.00	$	$	$	$370.00	5-10%	10%
Credit Cards	$120.00					$120.00		
Student Loans		$250.00				$250.00		
Personal/401k Loans						$		
Giving	$	$	$	$	$	$		0%
Charitable Giving (religious, private charity)						$		
Fees	$	$	$	$	$	$		0%
Bank/Credit Union Account Fees						$		
Professional Services Fees						$		
Clothing	$	$	$	$	$	$	4-6%	0%
Clothing (family)						$		
Uniforms, accessories for work						$		

							2-8%	3%
Entertainment/Recreation	$	$100.00	$	$	$	$100.00		
Entertainment/Activities		$100.00				$100.00		
Subscriptions/Dues						$		
Fitness /Spa						$		
Pets	$	$	$	$	$	$		0%
Food, grooming, etc.						$		
Veterinarian, pet insurance						$		
Miscellaneous	$	$	$	$	$	$		0%
Toiletries/Cosmetics/grooming						$		
Professional Membership Dues/Fees						$		
Other						$		
Investments	$	$	$	$	$	$		0%
Stocks, Bonds, CDs, Mutual Funds						$		
IRAs/Retirement						$		
Second Property Expenses						$		

TESTIMONY TIME: *Day 7*

Before the fast, I wasn't living on a budget and properly controlling the resources God had entrusted to my care. After the wakeup call I received by participating in the fast, I was consciously aware of the importance of a budget and my responsibility to control my spending by adhering to the biblical financial principles I knew to be right.

For anyone contemplating the financial fast, whether you're fiscally responsible or an out-of-control spender, I strongly encourage you to take the plunge, do the fast, and see how much of a difference it will make in your life!

Bethany

DAILY ASSIGNMENT

You know what to do. Follow all the instructions in the chapter to begin putting your budget together. You may not finish today, but you must begin the process today. By the end of Day 11, which is the end of Part 2, "Fasting for a Better Financial Life," you should have completed your budget. (You can find an online version of this budget at michellesingletary.com.)

Journal daily from now through Day 11 about your feelings concerning your budget. Use the sample journal entry in the appendix as a reference if you need help. Whatever you do, don't give up — even if the numbers look grim. Remember that God is with you during this entire process.

The Salvation of Saving

14 Days to Go: God's Blueprint for Saving

Main Point: There is great reward in saving.

My Pledge: I will commit today to set aside a percentage of every paycheck for my savings.

Would you be surprised to learn the US had seven years of plenty beginning in 2000? During these years of plenty:

- Debt consumption (people taking on new debt) rose, which helped pull the US economy out of the recession of 2000.

- Home values rose.

- The savings rate in the US was abysmal. In 2005, the national savings rate dipped below zero.

- Homeowners took advantage of low interest rates by borrowing against the seemingly never-ending rise in the value of their homes. They borrowed to pay for home improvements, college tuition, a car, or to roll the debt from a car into their mortgage. They borrowed against their homes to take vacations or pay off credit card debt.

- Rising home prices led families to concentrate more and more of their wealth into their homes even as they expanded their credit lines to maintain their consumption.

- During this time of plenty, many individuals didn't save.
- Many corporations weren't saving.
- The federal government increased its spending, eroding what had been a nice budget surplus.

For a time, it seemed as though the housing boom and economic expansion would go on for decades. People believed the value of their home would always go up.

By the end of 2007, the credit ride was over. The recession hit, and the wails of broke individuals and corporations kicked off one of the worst economic mudslides in decades. God sent seven years of plenty before what could be considered a modern-day famine.

If you know the Old Testament story of Joseph, you'll recall how Joseph interpreted Pharaoh's disturbing dreams — and saved an entire nation from starvation as a result. What I like about this biblical story is the blueprint we get for saving. Joseph relied on his faith to save even when times were plentiful. Year after year he stored up grain. He never wavered from his task, even when the grain was overflowing. "During the seven years of abundance the land produced plentifully. Joseph collected all the food produced in those seven years of abundance in Egypt and stored it in the cities. In each city he put the food grown in the fields surrounding it. Joseph stored up huge quantities of grain, like the sand of the sea; it was so much that he stopped keeping records because it was beyond measure" (Gen. 41:47 – 49).

There are two key parts of this passage in Genesis that I want to point out. First, Joseph was instructed to take a "fifth," or 20 percent, of all the harvest and set it aside for the future. Specifically this savings was to be reserved so that the country would not be ruined when the famine, or bad times, came — as it always has and will. Don't miss this important point. It is hard for us to save when times are good because we forget that there will always be bad times too. During good times we need to dig deep and find the discipline to save consistently as Joseph did.

Second, Joseph stored up so much grain, he had to stop counting. Wouldn't you like to have that problem? Wouldn't you like to have so much saved that you didn't even have to keep checking the balance? I want to also note that Joseph saved so much, when others in need came, he could help. "When the famine had spread over the whole country, Joseph opened all the storehouses and sold grain to the Egyptians, for the famine was severe throughout Egypt. And all the world came to Egypt to buy grain from Joseph, because the famine was severe everywhere" (Gen. 41:56 – 57).

> *"I spoke to you in your prosperity; but you said, 'I will not listen!' This has been your practice from your youth, that you have not obeyed My voice."*
>
> Jeremiah 22:21 NASB

In fact the abundance of food helped Joseph to reunite with his brothers. "When Jacob learned that there was grain in Egypt, he said to his sons, 'Why do you just keep looking at each other?' He continued, 'I have heard that there is grain in Egypt. Go down there and buy some for us, so that we may live and not die'" (Gen. 42:1 – 2).

If Joseph had not followed the dream interpretations given to him by God, there would have been no grain to give to his brothers or to others. Joseph would not have been used to bless so many, something he acknowledges when he finally reveals his identity to his brothers. "Then Joseph said to his brothers, 'Come close to me.' When they had done so, he said, 'I am your brother Joseph, the one you sold into Egypt! And now, do not be distressed and do not be angry with yourselves for selling me here, because it was to save lives that God sent me ahead of you'" (Gen. 45:4 – 5).

I honestly tear up when I read that last verse. Joseph's obedience saved the lives of many. He saved year after year after year of plenty. How many blessings are you missing because you spend every dime you make? Who are you failing to connect with and bless because you don't have enough to share because you've failed to save?

I know that saving isn't sexy. It isn't fun. It involves patience. It takes discipline. And yet the spiritual and worldly rewards are so great.

TESTIMONY TIME: *Day 8*

I made the very difficult decision to cancel a planned trip to Jamaica for my thirtieth birthday. I had always dreamed of a big vacation to celebrate this milestone birthday and had started saving money to pay for it.

The problem, however, was that I also wanted to buy a house. After giving it some serious thought, I realized that the vacation was a very temporary goal, while becoming a homeowner was a lifelong goal that also had long-term benefits for my family. I sent an email to all my friends who were already planning and saving for this trip with me and explained my decision. Surprisingly, every one of them congratulated me on this decision and gave me their full support.

Adrienne

TWO ESSENTIAL FUNDS

There are two major savings accounts you should have — an emergency fund and a "life happens" fund.

Emergency Fund: An emergency fund should hold a minimum of three to six months of living expenses. This should include your rent or mortgage payment and all expenses for cars, food, utilities, gas, and other ordinary household needs. You might as well throw cable into the calculation, as well as the average amount you spend eating out or for entertainment. Don't underestimate how much you need in an emergency. Even in a crisis it takes several months before the average family cuts back sufficiently on their expenses to accommodate a significant reduction in their income. If you are a highly paid individual or you think it may take a long time to find a job in your career area, boost your savings to cover expenses for six months to a year.

"Life Happens" Fund: You need to save for when things happen in life — the car breaks down, your kid busts the washing machine, your refrigerator dies, and so on. If you don't save for these expenses, you end up depleting your emergency fund, which should be reserved for dire situations, such as a job loss. How much you save in this account depends on your individual situation. If you have an older car that regularly needs repairing, save up enough for at least one large repair bill a year ($700 to $800). If you have children, they will break things ($250 to $500). Generally, I suggest you keep at least $1,000 in the "life happens" fund, but you might need to save more.

TESTIMONY TIME: *Day 8*

Our greatest savings plan is our "life happens" fund. It's our greatest not in terms of amount but in terms of peace of mind. It's the fund that is most useful because it keeps us out of debt.

Terri

You have several options for where to put your emergency fund and "life happens" fund. Keep in mind this isn't money you want to put at risk by, say, investing it in volatile stocks. This is money you want to keep in a safe, accessible place. Here are three good options:

Simple savings account. Even in a low-interest-rate environment you can find institutions offering better-than-average interest rates on a deposit savings account. But you may have to move beyond your comfort zone. Some of the best rates are not from typical brick-and-mortar banks. You may find the best deals at Internet-only institutions. Internet-only banks are governed by the same regulations as traditional banks and credit unions. However, since you can't see the people you're dealing with, check with the Federal Deposit Insurance Corporation (FDIC) before putting your money into one of these banks.

To search for institutions with the highest savings account rates, go to *www.bankrate.com*. When going with a nontraditional financial institution, check the fine print, because transfers can take a few days and you may be limited to a certain number of withdrawals a month.

But none of these terms should deter you. After all, this is your emergency money, and you don't want it to be too easy to withdraw.

Money-market deposit account. These are interest-earning savings accounts offered by FDIC-insured financial institutions. Money-market deposit accounts offer many of the same privileges as checking accounts, but you are limited in the number of transactions you can make in a month. These accounts have a minimum balance requirement. If you are going to use this type of account to hold your rainy-day money, be mindful of any monthly fee, especially if your balance drops below a designated amount. Also check to see whether you get a higher rate if you deposit a larger amount.

Certificates of deposit. Short-term CD rates can be low. The longer the CD, the better the rate. However, you don't want to lock up your emergency money for months at a time. You could "ladder" your CDs. Laddering allows you to take advantage of typically higher rates offered by longer-term CDs while maintaining access to some of your money. With this strategy, you divide your money and buy a series of CDs that mature at different times. For an online calculator to help you figure out how to ladder your money in CDs, visit *www.bankrate.com*. Look under the link for calculators.

I really want to emphasize the need to create a "life happens" fund. People get the concept of an emergency or rainy-day fund, and I know this second unique fund may not seem necessary or doable if you've got a tight budget. However, the "life happens" fund is essential. The money saved in this account will keep you from going into debt because of expenses that you really should be planning for. For example, one question I'm often asked is when should you buy a new car? People typically ask this question when they are faced with a major car repair. So the situation might be, "Should I pay $900 to fix an aging car or buy a new car?"

To which I ask, "What is more, $900 or $28,000 (the average price of a new car)?" Add on top of that the interest charges and higher insurance (for a new car), and the decision seems clear to me. Get the car fixed.

The problem is that people don't prepare for such things by saving, so they seek to solve the problem by borrowing. It's sad that people have to buy a new car because they don't have the money saved to fix the one they have. Equally frustrating to me is that the banking system has made it easier to borrow large sums of money. You may not be able to borrow $900 to fix your car, but you can borrow $28,000 to buy a new car. Instead of praying and asking God to find a way to keep the old car, people immediately turn to the auto lender.

This action is particularly troubling when someone is upside down on their car loan, meaning they owe more than the vehicle is worth. So to get a new car, they have to add the balance owed on the old car to that of the new car, increasing their debt.

They don't wait on God, or heed God's warnings about the importance of saving when times are good to cover their costs when the times are bad.

This is why it's important to have two rainy-day accounts — an emergency fund and a "life happens" fund. My grandmother, Big Mama, used to tell me that it's important to have a rainy-day fund because it's always going to rain. Having both an emergency and a "life happens" fund is like keeping an umbrella in your purse and car. They are there so that when it rains you have protection you can grab right away.

KNOW WHERE YOU STAND

Just about every morning, even before I brush my teeth, I get on the scale. I just have to know where I stand weight-wise — is it up or down? Knowing helps me eat healthier. The concern that my hips are spreading keeps me from eating the carrot cake that I love. Or it makes me skip buying the bag of potato chips that seems to call out my name as I pass it in the grocery store.

When it comes to your net worth, knowing where you stand — how much true wealth you have — can be the same kind of motivator for better managing your money.

Unfortunately, only about half (49 percent) of adults know what their personal net worth is. Your net worth is determined by adding up all your assets (household and personal possessions, cash in bank or credit union accounts, cash value built up in an insurance policy, retirement savings, plus the market value of your home) and deducting all your liabilities (what you owe on your home, credit cards, or other loans). There's a net worth statement for you to fill out at the end of this chapter. You can also go to *www.michellesingletary.com* and download an Excel version, which will do all the math for you.

Probably the biggest asset you'll list on your net worth statement is your house. With your house — the greatest source of many people's wealth — you deduct the amount you owe on your mortgage (liability) from the approximate fair market value of the property. If the resulting number shows your house is worth more than you owe, then you have equity, an asset, in the home.

When you take the time to list your assets, the exercise helps you see just where you might be able to find extra money should you lose or quit your job. Where would you get the money to sustain your household during a time of unemployment? Check your net worth statement.

THE GOSPEL OF FRUGALITY

My grandmother, Big Mama, preached the gospel of frugality during every economic upswing and downturn. She taught me to live as if there were always a recession. If you live as though prices will rise drastically tomorrow, you'll watch what you spend today at the grocery store. If you're wary about the direction of gas prices, you'll be more fuel efficient. You'll buy a car that gets good gas mileage. You'll drive less and more slowly.

If you live as though you could lose your job tomorrow, you'll spend less than you make. Big Mama worked twenty-five years for the same hospital as a nursing assistant and was never late to work. Her boss would have been a fool to get rid of one of the hardest-working employees at that hospital. And yet during those twenty-five years, my grandmother planned as if she would be fired at any time. She had enough saved to pay her bills for a while if she ever did lose her job and needed time to find another one.

If you think the way my grandmother did, you would put something — anything — away in an emergency fund. If you live as if your job is constantly in jeopardy, you wouldn't see every raise or bonus as a chance to consume more.

If you live in a mental recession, you would reject the advice that there is good debt and bad debt. There isn't. There is only debt.

Some debt is necessary. Only a privileged few in this country can buy a home with cash. Still, if you live like you are in the midst of a recession, you see debt as a drag on your finances and mental health. And if you view all debt this way, then you will be very cautious about how much you take on, even to buy a home. You'd adopt the mantra "No debt is good debt." If you live in a mental recession, you won't view your home as an ATM. You won't extract equity to finance a car or pay college expenses.

You would have the common sense not to listen to advice from financial professionals who urge people — young and old, rich, middle class, and poor — to leverage debt to become wealthy. You won't dare borrow to invest.

If you live as if a recession were looming, you wouldn't see credit as an extension of your income. You wouldn't charge anything you couldn't pay off the next month. People who have lived through tough economic times know that the less strain you have on your income from debt payments, the better you can weather a financial storm.

Let me be clear: Don't live in fear. There is a difference between a mental recession and a state of panic. Living in a mental recession pulls you back from spending too much. It encourages you to save. However, people end up panicking because they haven't planned or saved. That lack of provision makes them fearful, and that can separate them from God. Remember, God promises not to forsake us.

I love saving. I always have. It gives me peace. Saving can't always protect you from every financial disaster, but it certainly can help you weather them a bit better. No matter what you earn, resolve to set aside something, even if it's just $5 per paycheck. There's power in saving.

DAILY ASSIGNMENT

*If you are not regularly saving money, make the commitment today to save at least **5 percent** of every paycheck. For example, if your net income during one pay period is $1,500, you will save $75.*

If you work for a company, contact your benefits coordinator to set up an automatic deposit into your savings account. Put the money into an account and resolve not to touch it.

If you are already saving, consider increasing the amount you are putting aside. Five percent is just a beginning. If you really want to boost your savings, go for 10 or 15 percent.

To give your savings a purpose, list the things you would like to do with the money. For example, pay off a debt, take a long-overdue vacation, make some home improvements, etc. Post the list someplace where you will see it frequently to help maintain your commitment and motivation to save.

NET WORTH STATEMENT

ASSETS	CURRENT VALUE
Cash in Savings Accounts	
Cash in Checking Accounts	
Certificates of Deposit (CDs)	
Cash on Hand	
Money-Market Accounts	
Cash Value of Life Insurance	
Savings Bonds (current value)	
College Fund (529 plans, other accounts)	
Stocks	
Bonds	
Mutual Funds	
Vested Value of Stock Options	
Other Investments	
Individual Retirement Accounts (IRAs, ROTH)	
Other retirement accounts (Keogh, SEP, etc.)	
401(k) or 403(b) Accounts	
Current Market Value of Your Home *http://realestate.yahoo.com/Homevalues*	
Market Value of Other Real Estate	
Blue Book Value of Cars / Trucks (go to *www.kbb.com*)	
Boats, Planes, Other Vehicles	
Jewelry	
Collectibles	
Furnishings and Other Personal Property	
Other (money owed to you)*	
TOTAL ASSETS	

* Include only if you reasonably expect to collect!   *(Table continued)*

LIABILITIES	CURRENT VALUE
Mortgages (total owed)	
Home Equity Loan	
Home Equity Line of Credit	
Auto Loans	
Credit Card Balances	
Bank / Credit Union Loans	
401(k) / 403(b) / Thrift Savings Plan Loan	
Student Loans	
Other Loans	
Outstanding Real Estate Taxes Owed	
Federal or State Income Taxes Owed	
Other Taxes Owed	
Other Debts (business, personal)	
TOTAL LIABILITIES	
NET WORTH (TOTAL ASSETS MINUS TOTAL LIABILITIES)	

A net worth statement is just a snapshot of your current financial situation. Please keep in mind that the value of your assets can change, as many homeowners have found out in the current mortgage crisis.

Diversification Delivers

13 Days to Go: Investing for Your Future

Main Point: Understand that when you invest, you put your money at risk.

My Pledge: I will examine my investments to make sure I'm well diversified.

For much of the fast, you've been focused on why you should curtail your spending or cut your credit usage, but today we'll spend some time thinking about how to make your money grow. I want to talk to you about investing.

Part of being a good steward is making sure you can buy the things you need (or even want) in the future. One of the biggest threats to your financial well-being is inflation. Beating inflation means making sure your dollars today can purchase the things you need tomorrow — gas, food, utilities, etc. If you have children who will someday attend college, you should be saving for that. And everyone should be investing to help with their own retirement.

If you have investments, open up your statements and take a look. Some people follow their portfolios carefully; others figure if they don't see the money, they won't touch it. I understand the latter point of view, but you can't just close your eyes and wish for the best.

Depending on what the stock market is doing, you may feel pretty whiplashed. Certainly over the years the stock market has left people wondering if it's better to just stuff their cash in a mattress. (It's not.)

If you are investing through your employer's retirement plan, such as a 401(k), go online to view your portfolio or get your most recent quarterly statement. Look at where and how you've allocated your money. Is it spread across various asset classes? Or have you concentrated your contributions in just one or two types of investments? In other words, is your money all in one basket or is it diversified?

Ecclesiastes 11:2 affirms the importance of diversification, saying, "Invest in seven ventures, yes, in eight; you do not know what disaster may come upon the land." King Solomon, who is considered one of the wisest men ever to have lived, encourages investment in seven or eight ventures. Why? You invest in more than one venture so that if any one fails, you have the others to rely on for funds.

Diversification delivers safety and is the key to minimizing investment losses. As an investor, you want to give your money both time to grow and time to weather the ups and downs that can happen in each asset area. For example, when the returns for stocks are up, bonds are typically down. Also, home values don't always go up. If you concentrate all your wealth in only one of those areas, you could face losses.

If you stockpile too much cash because you are too afraid to invest, you risk losing your purchasing power to inflation. The inflation rate has averaged between 3 and 4 percent over the last twenty years or so, according to the Bureau of Labor Statistics. In a low-interest savings account you'd actually be losing value on your money over time.

If you put all your money in one type of asset, you increase your risk because you may not be able to sell the asset to raise needed cash. That's what happened to many homeowners when the recession hit in 2007. They had so much of their money locked into their homes that when housing prices began to sink, they couldn't sell their homes for enough to cover their mortgages.

UNDERSTANDING ASSET ALLOCATION

You've probably heard the expression, don't put all your eggs into one basket. Intuitively you may know what that means — to diversify. But practically it means having cash, stocks, and bonds. It means spreading your money among those three major asset classes.

When you diversify, all you're really doing is hedging against an unknown future. It's like using crutches after you break your leg. You have to distribute your weight just right to keep from falling or putting too much pressure on any one side of your body. The same is true with your money.

You have to be strategic about accumulating cash, stocks, and bonds. If the distribution of any one of those areas is off target, you could fall.

If you stockpile too much cash because you are too afraid to invest, you risk losing your purchasing power to inflation. If you put all your money in one type of asset, you risk losing money because you can't sell the asset to raise needed cash. Following is a breakdown of each asset class:

Stocks. A stock represents a share of ownership in a corporation. Stock price appreciation (growth) is based on a company's dividends and profits and how investors assess the corporation's potential for future profits. Historically, stocks have provided the highest returns over time, but stock prices fluctuate — sometimes dramatically. Included in this category are various equities: large-cap (or big companies); mid-cap (medium-size companies); small cap (small or upstart companies); and stock shares in international companies. Most people are familiar with stocks through their mutual fund. Mutual funds pool money from thousands, even millions, of investors to buy stocks, as well as bonds, other securities, and mixtures of securities. For that stock-picking service, mutual fund shareholders pay a range of fees, including a management fee to the fund managers who decide which stocks to buy. There are thousands of mutual funds with different investment strategies and vastly different rates of return.

Bonds. Bonds are IOUs issued by governments, government agencies, and corporations. Interest-rate changes directly affect the prices and returns of bonds, but in general, bond prices fluctuate less than those of stocks. Investors typically choose bonds, which are also referred to as fixed income, to balance out the risk of investing in stock portfolios.

Cash. Finally, there is plain old cash and cash equivalents, which are very short-term IOUs issued by a government, corporation, bank, or other financial institution. Money-market mutual funds (different from the money-market accounts, which, up to a limit, are always protected by the FDIC) try to maintain a stable price of $1 a share. If you have questions about insurance the government provides for your cash holdings, go to *www.myfdicinsurance.gov*. On the site you will find EDIE, a calculator that will tell you how much of your cash in a bank account is covered by the Federal Deposit Insurance Corporation. I've always diversified my cash holdings between various institutions. I've done that partly because I was raised by a grandmother who lived through the Great Depression. Like Big Mama, I also spread my cash around because I don't like having all of my money at one financial institution.

For our regular household accounts, my husband and I use a bank with a large ATM network because we travel a lot and we don't want

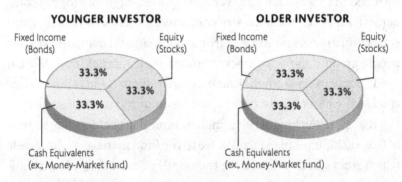

| YOUNGER INVESTOR | OLDER INVESTOR |

Fixed Income (Bonds) — Equity (Stocks) — 33.3% — 33.3% — 33.3% — Cash Equivalents (ex., Money-Market fund)

Fixed Income (Bonds) — Equity (Stocks) — 33.3% — 33.3% — 33.3% — Cash Equivalents (ex., Money-Market fund)

Source: The Financial Industry Regulatory Authority (www.finra.org)

to pay ATM fees. We have a credit union account where we keep cash for large purchases or major repairs. The cash in the credit union is also designated as our "life happens" fund. We created this fund to avoid draining our emergency cash, which we reserve for dire situations. We use a money-market mutual fund account to hold some of our emergency cash.

An investment in knowledge always pays the best interest.

Benjamin Franklin

When it comes to investing, here are some general (very general) guidelines on how you might invest based on your age.* The first pie chart on the opposite page is an example of how a young investor, decades away from retirement, might invest. The second chart is a sample asset allocation for someone closer to retirement or in retirement. You might still want to have money invested in the stock market even during retirement because you don't want to outlive your money.

The closer you are to needing your money, the less risk you may want to tolerate. Greg Womack, a certified financial planner, recommends that if you are retiring in five years or less, you should have already built up five years' worth of income in safe investments, so when you do retire, you won't need to panic if there is a downward spiral in the stock market. If you have money to live on that is not at risk, you are better able — assuming you can handle the risk — to leave a portion of your portfolio in the market to recover and have potential to grow.

Here's an example from Womack of how to figure out what you'll need for retirement. Let's say you are 60 years old and have a 401(k) plan with a $300,000 balance. You want an annual income at 65 of

---

* Note that these percentages are suggestions only and will vary on a number of factors, including how much risk you are willing to tolerate and what goals you have. For more information on investing, go to *www.finra.org/Investors/index.htm*, a website run by the Financial Industry Regulatory Authority (FINRA), the largest nongovernmental regulator for all securities firms doing business in the United States. For seniors or military members, FINRA has developed an investor education website at *www.saveandinvest.org*.

$60,000. Subtract any other sources of fixed income (i.e., social security, pension, etc.). For example, if social security will provide $22,000 a year, that means you'll need an additional $38,000 per year from your personal investments. Five years at $38,000 = $190,000. This is the amount to save and preserve in safe accounts.

The bottom line is that you need to review your investments to determine if you are adequately diversified based on your tolerance for risk and your financial goals. Here are a few guidelines to help you hedge against future financial risk and to ensure diversification not just in your investment portfolio but in all of your financial holdings.

TESTIMONY TIME: *Day 9*

I started my first financial fast (in 2005), and I still maintain the lifestyle to this day.
Impulse buying does not pull me anymore. The fast has made me genuinely happy! One more little tidbit as a result of the shift: The Lord has blessed me to always have a substantial offering to give back for kingdom building.

Angela

Maintain a cash reserve. Cash is and will always be king. We certainly learned the importance of having cash after the 2007 recession hit. How much cash you should have depends on your individual situation. For instance, if you're a highly compensated individual and you think you might lose your job, you might consider saving six months to a year's worth of living expenses because it's probable that it will take that long to replace your high salary.

Get adequate insurance coverage. Insurance hedges your bet against an expense you can't possibly save for in the short term, such as a disability or the death of the family breadwinner. Talk to a professional to make sure you have enough disability insurance and life insurance. For a good, independent source of information on life insurance, go to *www.insureuonline.org*, a website created by the National Association of Insurance Commissioners.

Allocate assets wisely. Don't dump all your money into real estate, a single company stock, or any one particular investment. For example, when the stock market takes a dive, many unsophisticated investors rush to buy gold. While gold can be a good addition to your portfolio, you shouldn't be overexposed in this asset class. It's not like you can take a bar of gold or a gold chain and buy some milk if need be. For that, you still need cash. You can find some basic information about asset allocation at the Securities and Exchange Commission's website at *www.sec.gov/investor/pubs/assetallocation.htm.* I've also found a particularly helpful asset allocation tutorial at *www.investopedia.com.* Search for "A Guide to Portfolio Construction."

Never borrow to invest. It is not wise to borrow money to invest. When it comes to investing in anything — stocks, bonds, or real estate — you only invest what you can afford to lose. If you borrow to invest and the investment tanks, you are left with a loan.

Borrow strategically. If you have to take on debt, keep it to a minimum. For example, if you're married, don't have two car loans at the same time. I've seen household budgets where the combined car loans were almost equivalent to a mortgage or rent payment.

Being diversified can't save you from every financial disaster. Still, be sure to diversify, because to do otherwise is to make a huge gamble. Don't gamble on a single stock, bond, or asset if you can't afford the losses.

DAILY ASSIGNMENT

*Visit a website that explains the basics of investing. I've already listed several, but at least start with **www.finra.org** or **www.mymoney.gov**.*

Review your investment statements — including your retirement account and your children's college fund. Look at where and how you've allocated the money in your 401(k) or other retirement plans. Is it spread across various asset classes? Or have you concentrated your contributions in just one or two types of asset categories? In other words, is your money all in one basket?

*If you are not investing, make the commitment today to begin investing for your future. If you are eligible for a 401(k) plan at your job, start contributing to it. If your employer doesn't provide a retirement plan, resolve to invest anyway. You can open an IRA. To find out more information about an IRA, go to **www.investorprotection.org**. Read "Maximize Your Retirement Investments." You can also find information on how to open an IRA at **www.choosetosave.org**.*

Marrying Your Money

12 Days to Go: It's Not Just about You

Main Point: Together as one you can become better stewards of your money.

My Pledge: I will work with my spouse to develop a set of rules to govern how we handle our money together.

When you're single, you have complete freedom to decide what to do with your finances. However, one of the blessings of being in a marriage is that the whole is greater than the sum of the parts. One plus one can equal more than two!

If you're single, don't be tempted to skip over this chapter and lessons for the day. You may never get married, but then again, God may have a mate for you. Knowing how to handle your money within a marriage will be important to having a successful relationship.

When you're married, it can't be about yours and mine; it's got to be about *ours!* You are working together to be good stewards over the riches and wealth that God has gifted to you both. If you stay mindful of this fact, then selfishness can't even enter into your marriage relationship. One of the hardest and saddest things I encounter in my ministry is couples who are not in one accord with their finances. They fight or argue over whether or not to have joint accounts (which you should). They fight over spending. They fight because they don't have a budget. Far too often, feuding couples let money get in the way of building their wealth.

TESTIMONY TIME: *Day 10*

My wife and I were not in one accord in our spending habits, and she didn't trust that the fast was a means to financial freedom. As we know, when one half of the union does not agree, the fast can be difficult.

After meeting with a Senior Partner, we felt there was hope for us. By virtue of being obedient to God and to the fast, we were able to see his blessings and applied $13,000 to our debt within the first three to five months of being in the ministry.

Alton

FAMILIAR FIGHTS

It's often said that money is the main cause of marital discord and even divorce.

But that's not quite accurate. What really causes the fights is all the emotional baggage — fear, mistrust, immaturity, selfishness, or lack of self-worth — that gets stirred up when money enters the conversation. Money — that's just a convenient, albeit huge, catalyst for the quarrels.

One major problem with modern-day marriages is that people go into the union behaving like roommates, not lifetime partners as the Bible describes: "Therefore a man shall leave his father and mother and be joined to his wife, and they shall become one flesh" (Gen. 2:24 NKJV). Couples intellectually know — or should know — that God says we should become one flesh, yet somehow they don't think that applies to having joint bank accounts. They don't think that means sharing all their financial information with their spouse. They try to divide up everything as if they are living with a roommate. I know that's what I had planned on doing before I was married.

I wanted to go into my marriage with *seven* different bank accounts:

- My savings account
- His savings account
- My checking account
- His checking account
- A joint savings account
- A joint checking account
- A "home-wrecking hussy" account; you know, in case he ran off with some home-wrecking hussy

The idea for that last account came from my grandmother, Big Mama. She told me that every woman needed to keep some of her own money in her own secret bank account. As much as I loved my grandmother, she was wrong. And if you are keeping an account secret from your spouse, you're wrong too.

Here's a biblical principle that will bring peace to your house: "Do nothing out of selfish ambition or vain conceit. Rather, in humility value others above yourselves, not looking to your own interests but each of you to the interests of the others" (Phil. 2:3 – 4). Let's take a closer look at some key phrases in that passage.

Selfish ambition. Selfish ambition is never a good thing, and it's especially destructive in a marriage. Selfish ambition is looking out for oneself in a greedy way. One plus one can equal more than two in a marriage, but that kind of math means taking the focus off yourself and working as a team. You can't work as a team if one member is off doing his or her own thing financially.

Vain conceit. Vain conceit is never going to show up on a list of admirable character traits. Conceit is an inflated sense of self-importance, and vain conceit is pride and arrogance on steroids. Are you guilty of being conceited in your marriage, focusing on what you make, what you're worth? Are you spending on the things you want regardless of how that spending is affecting your family?

This would be a much better world if more married couples were as deeply in love as they are in debt.

Earl Wilson

Value others. Do you value your spouse's worth to the marriage? Do you hold her or him in high esteem? Do you listen to your spouse as directed in Proverbs 1:5, "Let the wise listen and add to their learning, and let the discerning get guidance"? When you value your spouse, you want to share with him or her all the financial information that will help you both achieve financial freedom. This is particularly important for the stay-at-home mother or father. Since we know that people attach their self-worth to their earning power, it's vital that you communicate the value you see in your spouse's work at home.

Not looking to your own interests. Are you looking out only for yourself in your marriage? Is your refusal to stick to a budget ruining your family's chance at prosperity?

All of the above are important questions you need to address during this day of the fast. Reflect on whether you've been selfish by neglecting to manage the money you earn in a way that will bless your family. Even if you and your spouse are determined to keep separate accounts and divvy up the bills, you still need to plan on how all the funds will be used. You shouldn't just pay your share of the bills and watch while your spouse scrimps and suffers under massive consumer or student loan debt. That's looking out for your own selfish interest to the detriment of your family. Instead, work together to pay the bills and retire debt no matter who brought it into the marriage. In fact, if you want to know how to work together, keep reading.

HOUSE RULES

For the longest time my husband and I have been preaching to couples about establishing and honoring "House Rules." Think about it this way. You follow rules for just about every aspect of your life. You have rules at your job that you must abide by. When you get behind the wheel of the car, for the most part, you obey the traffic laws (or pay the price if you don't). Yet when it comes to the most important relationship in your life, it's anarchy—every man for himself, every woman for herself. Or, you establish rules, but one or both of you break them regularly. For example, you may agree to stick to a budget, but instead you bust it every chance you get. You both may decide to limit your ATM withdrawals, but you decide that it's okay for you to violate that rule when it suits you.

To get you started on developing your own "House Rules," here are a few policies that should be standard in your marriage:

Rule No. 1: Agree that neither of you can make a purchase above a certain amount of money without first consulting each other. If you're just starting out and not earning much, then that agreed-upon amount may be as low as $20. If you are both well paid, you might set the amount at perhaps $200. Just be careful of setting the amount too high. The point of this rule is to be intentional about discussing your spending, and to avoid spending more than the agreed-upon amount without discussion.

Rule No. 2: Agree that there will be no financial secrets, no secret bank accounts, no earnings that are not disclosed, no undisclosed loans, no hidden purchases, and no secret credit cards. Think of it this way—when two businesses merge, there is complete disclosure of all assets. The same should be the case for your marriage.

Rule No. 3: Once you marry, it should take two "Yeses" and one "No" for any major financial decision. That means if one of you disagrees with a purchase or an investment, the other can't go ahead with it.

Rule No. 4: Join all your finances. For the most part, you should have joint bank accounts. And for goodness' sake, why haggle over who is responsible for various household bills? That's what roommates do. They divvy up the expenses. In a marriage your debts, assets, cash, and income must all be shared. Often the whole idea of having separate accounts is to be able to pick up and leave the marriage with your stuff should you divorce. That's planning for failure. That's operating out of fear. And the Bible says there is no fear in love (1 John 4:18).

Again, once you marry you mustn't act like roommates who live together and operate their financial lives separately. Instead act as if you are life mates and operate your financial lives together with one plan.

TESTIMONY TIME: *Day 10*

The fast was a learning experience about willpower. I didn't want to do the fast, but because of pressure from my wife, I succumbed and dealt with it. Here's what happened:

1. I could not go to the supermarket unless I wanted to hear the wrath of my wife.

2. I did not want to be restricted on what I could and could not purchase, much like everyone else, I assume.

3. I learned that most of my wants were just that—wants—and were not necessary.

4. I saved money.

5. I knew deep down in my gut that this was the right thing to do, but you know that old sense of "entitlement" tried to rear its ugly head and get in the way.

6. It made me aware of my money and what to spend it on.

7. The little treats of going to the theater or renting movies were nipped but not so significantly that we could not live without them. Lord knows we did not need to spend any money at those concession stands.

All in all, I have no regrets to speak of. But I do not want to make this a regular task, even though I know it is a necessary evil!

Larry

DAILY ASSIGNMENT

If you are married (or engaged, as in there's a ring and a firm date set), work together to come up with at least ten "House Rules" to handle your money as a couple. I've already started you off with four, so you have only six more to go. Once you are in agreement, write down the rules. I mean it. Put them on paper and keep the rules handy so there is no question what you both agreed to.

Read Luke 14:28. Discuss with your spouse what this Scripture passage means. Here's a hint: The passage is about the importance of planning.

If you are not married, make a list of the financial qualities you would like to have in a mate. Now, create a list of the financial issues you have and would like to improve upon before getting married.

Leave a Legacy of Good Money Sense

11 Days to Go: Children Live What They Learn

Main Point: Train your child to be a good money manager.

My Pledge: I will show my child by example what it means to be a good steward over money.

Train up children in the way they should go, as the Scripture says, and when they are old, they will not depart from it.

Somehow that lesson gets lost for many families when it comes to teaching children about money. There certainly isn't a lack of resources for any parent who wants to teach their child good money management habits. A number of government agencies, nonprofits, and private companies promote financial literacy and produce useful educational material for kids.

As parents, we know it's imperative to teach our kids to say no to drugs and alcohol. But can you honestly say you're doing your best to help them fend off consumerism and credit card pushers?

Your children probably won't find a path to prosperity unless you show them. But so many parents don't know how to say no to their kids, giving them all that they ask for, or allowing them to lead a life they can't sustain in their early adult lives. We may be spoiling our children's chances of growing into responsible adults.

I had a grandmother tell me once, "It's my job to spoil my grandson."

Really?

Because this is the definition of *spoil*: to damage seriously, to impair the disposition or character of by overindulgence or excessive praise.

> *The best time to start giving your children money is when they will no longer eat it. Basically, when they don't put it in their mouths, they can start putting it in their bank.*
>
> Barbara Coloroso

Don't skip today's lesson if you don't have children. Is there a child in your life who you can help become a better money manager — a niece, nephew, cousin, little sister or brother? It really does take a village to raise a child.

Perhaps when you saw the chapter title, you thought I might just be concentrating on leaving money to children. But that's not my focus for today's financial fast message. There is something more important that you can pass on to your children and your children's children — a legacy of good money sense.

Parents, you can say all the right things concerning money management, but you reproduce who you are and what you live. If you want to raise a money-smart kid, you have to live the life you want them to emulate.

TESTIMONY TIME: *Day 11*

About two years ago my mother confronted me about a few changes that she thought we should make in our lifestyle. She told me that she wanted to start a budget and a savings account and really evaluate the way we spend our money. At first I thought it was a great idea because I knew that it was important to my mother and I honestly thought it would not affect me. I just thought it meant no more excessive things and luxuries and that I would be okay with that. That was until I actually found out what luxuries were.

My mother was serious. Things she considered luxuries slowly disappeared. No more cable or eating out every night. Not that it was terrible, but it just wasn't what I was used to. I got bored with just fifteen channels on the television.

My mother showed me the budget, and for the first time I really realized that money didn't grow on trees. She showed me that we didn't have hundreds of dollars to spend on frivolous, unimportant things. But she also showed me the $600 in savings we had, and I could tell that was a big step for her and for us.

It was important that she shared the budget with me so I could really understand why we were making the changes we were and that it was for the better. I also realized that the real world wasn't what I thought. You have to be responsible and careful with your money, and rent is not a small expense. Since we've had a budget, I have tried to spend my money better, and I am sure that I will have a budget when I get older.

Now I don't just ask for random things when we are in the store. I know it's important to be smart with your money and that sometimes you have to sacrifice to be better off in the long run.

Jasmine, age 15

YOUR PRESENCE COUNTS

When my son was younger I recall asking him what he wanted for his birthday.

"I want my cousins Jordan, Kamryn, Lauren, Aunt Monique, Aunt Karen, Uncle Ronnie, Pop Pop, Olivia, Jillian, Mommy, and Daddy," he answered.

I didn't think he understood what I meant. So I repeated the question.

"I told you already. Oh, yeah, cake, hats, and plates. That's it," he said.

I tried asking a few more times until I realized that what my son wanted most was what money couldn't buy. All he really wanted was for his family to come together to celebrate his birthday.

That conversation reminded me that all he really wanted and needed — what all children need — is love, attention, acceptance, friends, and family. So many parents are not saying no to their kids.

They're giving them all that they ask for, when saying no is the best thing for them. We may be spoiling our children's chances of growing into responsible adults. "The student is not above the teacher, but everyone who is fully trained will be like their teacher" (Luke 6:40). In other words, teach and live a better financial life; you'll increase the likelihood your children will be good money managers.

God expects us to work, pay our bills, and take financial responsibility for ourselves and our families. This does not mean that we need to give our children everything they desire or everything we didn't have as children.

TESTIMONY TIME: *Day 11*

Because of your guidance, tough love, and godly principles, I am out of debt except for my mortgage, and my husband and I are working to pay that off.

My children's college funds have grown, as have my emergency fund and savings fund. I spend according to my budget, which I look at daily. The stress and worry of money no longer consume me. Something that was a daily worry is now a thing of the past.

Germaine

LIVING LARGE

Are you training your children to live on an average salary as young adults? Or are they living so large based on your income that they will be incapable of managing their finances on a modest starting salary once they stop living under your roof?

According to one survey, teens expect to make big bucks when they reach adulthood. The problem is that most won't earn anywhere near what they expect — at least in their early adult years. That disconnect is part of the reason why there are so many adults in credit card trouble or struggling to manage mortgages on homes they can't afford.

American teens believe that when they get older they will be earning an average annual salary of $145,500, according to the findings of a Teens and Money survey by Charles Schwab and the Boys & Girls Clubs of America. Only about 14 percent of US households have incomes between $100,000 and $200,000, according to the US Census Bureau. The median household income in the United States is less than $50,000.

Surveys like the one done by Schwab show a troubling trend. Many college students won't know how to get by on what they make once they graduate. Subtract local, state, and federal taxes and add in student loan and credit card debt, and our young people will have a lot less to live on than they're expecting.

It's fine that teens hope to earn high incomes, but just in case things don't turn out as they planned, you've got to teach them to live within their means. That's key because there's a level of financial confidence among young people that doesn't reflect what they actually know about money management.

Many teens certainly aren't learning to budget from their parents. They don't know how to pay bills, understand how credit card interest and fees work, or whether a check cashing service is good to use (it's not).

What they do know how to do is spend. They have no problem using credit. Teens are more likely to have a cell phone than a savings account.

In your journal for today, I want you to estimate the amount of time your teen or young child has spent at the mall with you compared to how much time you've spent talking to him or her about budgeting, saving, or investing. Would you be embarrassed to show anyone the difference? Children are going to practice what they experience. If they use shopping as a source of entertainment while they are young, they will likely continue that practice as adults. If you are not good with money, get better and then teach your children how to avoid the mistakes that you made. The greatest influence in your child's life isn't the media or their peers. It's you! If you don't have children, borrow a friend's or relative's child to help. Or take on a young adult to mentor.

Your children will have a better chance to live within their means as adults if you spend time showing them how to handle money when they're young. Teach them how to create a budget. I've already given you a template. At the end of this chapter I've created a simpler version for your child. Do your budget first and then work with them on theirs.

Right now, too many parents are teaching their children this: They want, you give. It will be hard for them to depart from that habit once they've grown up.

SAVING FOR COLLEGE

I don't want this day of the fast to go by without at least discussing the one inheritance you definitely should try to leave your child — a debt-free college education.

As my pastor says, "Don't look at me with that tone of face."

If you're a parent, I'm sure you read that statement and said, "This woman is out of her mind! I can't afford college for my child without going into debt."

I want to challenge that premise. I want to challenge you to reject the push to borrow whatever it takes to send your child to college. I want to challenge you to find a way to send your child off into his or her adult years without the bondage of student loans. For the first time in 2012, student-loan debt hit $1 trillion in outstanding debt, according to the Consumer Financial Protection Bureau and the Department of Education. A study by Fidelity Investments found that 70 percent of the class of 2013 graduated with debt averaging $35,200, which includes federal, state, and private loans, as well as debt owed to family and accumulated on credit cards.

It's become conventional wisdom that the debt accumulated for a college education is a good investment — "good" debt. But the truth is, it's just plain debt — and if you aren't careful, it will take decades to pay off that debt. I know. I've seen it. I've fielded the questions from parents with their own student loans struggling to pay the loans they've accumulated sending their children to college. They are now questioning the wisdom that college at any price is a guarantee to a good life, especially in an economy with high unemployment and lower starting salaries for college graduates. Between 2007 and 2010, the average student-loan balance for households increased almost 15 percent, even as Americans reduced other types of consumer debts, according to the Consumer Financial Protection Bureau. The National Association of Consumer Bankruptcy Attorneys has warned that a student-loan "debt bomb" would be America's next mortgage-style economic crisis.

Every parent knows that college costs are painfully high, and yet so many who could save, fail to save anything, even a small amount that will get their children through one semester or buy books. Instead, they wait until their children are ready to go to college, panic, and then turn to loans.

The other reality is that many people can't save to send their child to college because there isn't much money left over after essential expenses are paid. College is a hurdle many can't jump over.

Still, I know it's hard to deny your child her wish to attend a certain university when she's done all the right things — gotten good grades, stayed away from drugs, boys, and so on. When she says, "I'll die if I can't go to this school," she thinks she means it, and that presses on your heart to give in. (As you know, teenagers have the tendency to be overly dramatic about such things.)

Then there is the peer pressure, and not just from your child's friends. Tell the truth. Isn't there some vanity in your being able to say your child got into a brand-name school or the top state university?

You have to avoid the temptation of overspending for college. If you know it's going to be a struggle financially, manage your child's college expectations. Before your child settles on a particular school, underscore what's in your financial range. As an example, here are the two rules we've told our children:

1. *You can apply to any college you like.* We want them to explore all their options.

2. *You cannot go to a college if you or we have to borrow.* If any one of them is accepted to an expensive school, they have to earn scholarships to make up the difference between the fees and what we've already saved for their education. This rule helps keep the emotional factor in check when it comes to picking a college.

In the Fidelity survey, half of 2013 graduates with student loans said their level of debt surprised them. They hadn't realized how much they had borrowed. Thirty-nine percent said that if they had been aware of how much they would owe, they would have made different choices in their college planning.

Before you borrow or if you've already borrowed, you'll find some helpful information on the Consumer Financial Protection Bureau website: *www.consumerfinance.gov/students/.* This consumer watchdog agency has launched a very useful "Know Before You Owe" student loan project. On the website, you'll find information about paying for college, on repaying student loan debt if you've already borrowed or are still resigned to borrow. The site also helps borrowers with loan complaints.

Here's a question I often ask people when I speak to large groups: I ask everyone if they work with people who have gone to the priciest schools, state schools, or even community colleges. Almost everyone raises his or her hand. Then I ask: "Where do you all work?"

People laugh. But I'm serious.

They all ended up at the same workplace, often earning similar salaries. Yes, maybe for some, attending an elite school is the ticket to a high-profile, high-earning job. However, after a while, does it really matter what college you attended? Or is it, as many studies show, not so much about the school but about the person's drive?

Talk to your high school student early. You don't want to commit to writing a blank check for a college you or your child can't afford.

ONE WAY TO SAVE

If you've been following the fast, then you've likely discovered you can eke out some money in your monthly budget to set aside for a college fund for your kid. And I recommend investing that money in a 529 college savings plan.

There are two types of 529 plans: prepaid tuition plans and savings plans. A prepaid tuition plan allows you to pay a child's tuition in advance. The more popular savings plan allows you to invest in a tax-deferred investment account. Money withdrawn from a 529 investment is free from federal tax (and in most cases free from state and local taxes as well) when used for qualifying education costs.

Although the 529 plans are state sponsored, you can invest in any plan regardless of where you live. And money invested in a 529 plan can be used for a state or private institution. Every state and the District of Columbia now offer at least one 529 plan. The 529 plans operate much the way 401(k) retirement savings plans do. States, like employers, arrange for an investment company to set up and manage their 529 savings plans. Each plan can have a number of investment options. Just as with a 401(k), the money you invest is yours. You can take it out whenever you want. However, if you withdraw the money and it's not used for qualified higher education costs, your earnings may be subject to taxation and a 10 percent penalty.

There's an added bonus for many people who invest in their own state's 529 plan. In many states you can get a state income tax deduction. For example, in Maryland where I live, residents can get up to a $2,500 state tax break annually for each 529 savings account they have. If you're thinking about investing in a 529 savings plan, always check to see if your home state offers a tax break. This doesn't mean you should invest in that plan. It may turn out that the tax break isn't worth it when compared with the high expenses or poor performance of your state's savings plan.

Don't pay the price of procrastination. Whatever you can save to help with college expenses, do it now. Do it for your child's future.

BEFORE THEY DEPART

By the time children leave your house, there are some things they should know about money: how to live below their means, how to budget, how to save, and how to avoid debt. Oh, and they should also know how to write a check and balance their checkbooks.

How to live below their means. This means they need to know that they shouldn't be spending every penny they earn. Instill in your child that there are boundaries they must place on how money should be spent, and that spending must not exceed income.

How to budget. Teach them that the path to prosperity begins with a plan for their money. You should be saying to your kid, "Every penny has a purpose," until he or she threatens to put you in a nursing home if you don't stop.

How to save. Encourage them to save regularly. Talk to them about the importance of tithing. Teach them about having an emergency fund and a "life happens" fund.

How to avoid debt. Encourage your children to stay out of debt and to purchase with cash whenever possible. Discourage them from borrowing. If you've struggled with debt, share your pain with them. Let them know what it's like to be a slave to a lender.

Please take my advice and train your child well. If you don't, a debt counseling service will probably see them later.

Set an example by showing them that while holiday gifts are nice, they can enjoy life and their friends and family without an abundance of material things. Let your children "go without" sometimes. Don't overindulge them, especially if it's tapping you out. (Read the testimony below from one divorced mom who was going broke pleasing her children.)

Starting with whatever you can spare, begin to save for their college education. Help them start off life with as little debt as possible. Even if your income is limited, save *something*. At least enough to help them pay for books.

When we typically talk about leaving an inheritance to our children, we talk in terms of money. But I'm also talking about leaving your children with an inheritance that can never run out. Leave them with some good basic financial skills that will be passed on for generations.

TESTIMONY TIME: *Day 11*

The fast was very challenging. It made me realize how much money I spend unnecessarily on my kids. I am a single mother with two daughters, ages fourteen and ten. In the aftermath of a traumatic divorce, I found it very difficult to say no to my daughters. It was especially hard with my older daughter, who often asked for money to go to the mall with her friends or money to get her hair and nails done. She also broke our written agreement about her cell phone by sending emails and instant messages. This increased our bill to $350—an unaffordable amount for me.

After praying and meditating, I decided to have a talk with my daughters about our finances. I told them we were in financial difficulty. I explained why we needed to decrease our expenses and develop (and stick to) a budget. They both understood that it was more important for us to have our basic needs met—like having a home—rather than having a lot of material things. We also talked about our needs versus our wants.

The fast has not solved my problems, but it brought most of my issues to light. I now see the areas that I need to work on, and I am taking the necessary steps to improve in these areas.

Tamara

DAILY ASSIGNMENT

Estimate the amount of time your teen or young child has spent at the mall or shopping with you compared to how much time you've spent talking to him or her about budgeting, saving, or investing.

If you are embarrassed about how little time you've spent with your child or children talking about money, make a date to have a discussion. But make it fun. Come up with a creative way to talk about money. For example, if you have the game of Life or Monopoly, use it to begin a talk about managing money. If you don't have children, volunteer to do this exercise with a friend or relative's child.

Depending on the age of your child, let him or her do the shopping on your next grocery trip. The idea is to see how much they know about staying within the grocery budget (which of course means you need to have a list and a budget).

On the next page is a sample budget form you can use to practice showing your children how to manage their money. Also, you can go to michellesingletary.com to download a copy.

SAMPLE BASIC BUDGET WORKSHEET FOR TEENS

Income Source	Gross Income (Before Taxes)	Net Income (After Taxes)
Part-time job		
Babysitting / entrepreneurial effort		
Government benefit		
Allowance		
Total		

Expenses	Amount	Percentage of Net Income
Tithe and offering		
Transportation costs not covered by parent (insurance, gas)		
Cell phone		
School supplies / trips / clubs		
Grooming (beauty salon, barber)		
Clothing (items not purchased by parents or friends and relatives)		
Video / computer games		
Movies		
Eating out		
Miscellaneous		
Total Expenses		
Total Net Income		
Difference		

Your total expenses should be less than your net income. If there is money left over after expenses, encourage the child or teen to save it.

Part Three

FASTING TO AVOID FINANCIAL DRAMA

Congratulations! You are officially halfway through the fast! I hope you haven't given up. And if you've wavered, that's okay. Just regroup and keep going. It won't be long before it's over. Since you've persevered this far, you've proven that you've got grit — you can handle the tough stuff and stick it out. So now we're going to begin addressing some of the tougher issues. Yes, I said *tougher*. The five chapters in part 3 address the biggest barriers people face on the journey to achieving financial freedom. If you've been a devotee to debt or crushed by credit cards, these next few days are going to be challenging. You may feel convicted or challenged like never before in a lot of areas.

We're going to tackle paying down debt. I despise debt! Then we'll deal with the curse of credit, which probably tells you how I feel about that issue as well. I also have some choice things to say about the financial peril of co-signing a loan (it's crazy, so don't do it), and the dangers of giving into greed. Greed can make you a scam victim. This section also addresses the issues of caregiving. There are millions of caregivers struggling to figure out how to care for their aging loved ones without adequate financial resources. All the topics provide cautionary tales to help you avoid financial drama.

The Devil Is in the Debt

10 Days to Go: No Debt Is Good

Main Point: Debt is dangerous.

My Pledge: I will complete a debt reduction worksheet.

Now it's time to talk about how the devil is in the debt.

Debt is dangerous.

You can't get rid of your debt until you understand how having it and keeping it around can destroy your peace and happiness. In the song "Sixteen Tons," the lyricist writes, "Saint Peter don't you call me 'cause I can't go. I owe my soul to the company store." Do you feel that way sometimes, that you owe darn near everything to your creditors?

In modern times, debt seems to have become the latest tool used by the devil to entrap people and keep them from God's purpose for their lives. One survey by the Federal Trade Commission found that people with high levels of debt are also more likely to become victims of fraud. Almost one quarter of those who indicated that they had more debt than they could comfortably handle became victims of a variety of scams. Also those who felt that they had too much debt were more likely to have been victims of fraudulent prize promotions and foreign lottery scams. Many of these people are cheated because they became greedy trying to get great gains with little work. Greed (something I talk about later in this chapter) is just another form of coveting, and Scripture says, "The greedy bring ruin to their households" (Prov. 15:27).

TESTIMONY TIME: *Day 12*

During the fast I made up my mind that we were going to get out of debt after the mess I had gotten my family into. I had credit cards for the business that I didn't tell my husband about, and it hurt the family. I thought it was my business and I had it under control, but I didn't.

I did well on the fast after I made up my mind to be debt free. I am living better because I understand how God wants me to handle my money.

Renee

Americans have a love affair with debt. We want so much and we want it now! By the beginning of January 2009, one in ten mortgages was either delinquent or in foreclosure. The bust of the housing boom exposed just how comfortable we had become with debt. Like ripping an adhesive bandage off your arm, the housing crisis painfully exposed the fact that many of us were out of God's will when it came to the accumulation of debt. People falsely relied on the rising value of their homes to go on spending sprees, using debt when they should have been using savings. As their debt rose, people had to devote more of their income to servicing it. The US got into economic trouble because people were following the ideology of the capitalist market instead of abiding by Scripture.

WHAT DOES THE BIBLE SAY ABOUT DEBT?

I have yet to find a positive Scripture about debt. Everything I've ever read in the Bible about debt warns of its ability to enslave or bring darkness into your life.

Borrowing is not sin, but it puts you at a disadvantage. When you are in debt, you are beholden to someone else. Scripture warns against such a relationship. God's principles and debt are not compatible; they are unequally yoked.

Borrowing also puts you in the position of promising to pay for stuff before you've earned the money to pay for it. Scripture warns against such arrogance: "Do not boast about tomorrow, for you do not know what a day may bring" (Prov. 27:1). When you borrow, counting on income you haven't earned, you put yourself in a position of relying not on God but on the illusion of stability to help you honor your debts. This is a situation you should avoid or keep to a minimum.

The clearest warning in the Bible about being in debt is this: "The rich rule over the poor, and the borrower is slave to the lender" (Prov. 22:7). When you take on debt, you put yourself in bondage.

Visa once had an advertising slogan that said, "Life takes Visa." But ask yourself, is your Visa debt taking over your life? If you are in debt, then according to Scripture, you are a slave. If you are a slave, then you have a master. In fact, isn't that what many people have in MasterCard? Scripture says, "No one can serve two masters. Either you will hate the one and love the other, or you will be devoted to the one and despise the other. You cannot serve both God and money" (Matt. 6:24).

If you are a slave when you are in debt, what do you have if you don't have debt? Freedom. When you are released from debt, you are no longer beholden to someone else. You free up money to be used for the things you value. If you didn't have a mortgage, perhaps you could volunteer more in your community. You could increase your giving to the poor. You could spend more time with your family. You could travel. You could leave that job you hate and pursue a career that truly makes you happy. You could do so much more without the burden of carrying debt. God knows all of this, and it's why he cautions us about becoming burdened by debt.

IS THERE SUCH A THING AS GOOD DEBT?

There are two Chinese proverbs worth noting about debt: "A good debt is not as good as no debt," and "Free from debt is free from care."

No debt is good. But some debt may be necessary. Only a small percentage of Americans can purchase a house without a mortgage. But make no mistake about it, mortgage debt isn't good. It's only tolerable. Did you know that the word *mortgage* comes from the Old French *mort* meaning "dead," and *gage* meaning "pledge"? So, in essence, when you assume a mortgage, you are taking a death pledge. When you take on a mortgage, it certainly feels like " 'Til death do you part," doesn't it?

The same is true with student loan debt. This is not good debt, far from it, really. Student loans have become a crushing burden for many families. By the time they graduate, nearly two-thirds of students at four-year colleges and universities have student loan debt (66.4 percent in 2004). College graduates now face decades of student loan debt payments. More than half of former students in one student lender survey reported that they would have borrowed less if they had to do it over again.

If you still think a mortgage or a student loan is good debt, let me ask you this: What other words do you associate with *good*? Let me help you. How about:

Fine	Agreeable	Pleasant
Delightful	Enjoyable	

Now let me ask you another question: When it's time to make your monthly student loan or mortgage payment, do you feel fine about it? Are you in an agreeable mood? Is it pleasant? Are you so delighted that you enjoy writing the check or paying the bill online?

Be honest. You don't feel fine or agreeable, delighted, or even pleasant. In some cases the mere act of paying these bills makes some people want to cuss — and some do.

All debt puts you in bondage. Period. So don't listen when the world and the money changers try to convince you that there is good debt. As the apostle Paul says, "Do not conform to the pattern of this world, but be transformed by the renewing of your mind. Then you will be able to test and approve what God's will is — his good, pleasing and perfect will" (Rom. 12:2).

God's perfect will is for us to owe no one.

> *Be assured that it gives much more pain to the mind to be in debt, than to do without any article whatever which we may seem to want.*
>
> Thomas Jefferson in a 1787 letter to his daughter, Martha

BORROWING GUIDELINES

Clearly, there are circumstances in which you will have to borrow money. In the US we would have an extremely low homeownership rate if people had to wait until they saved up the entire amount before purchasing a home. You may have to borrow if you are in dire straits, such as if you lose a job and have to borrow from family and friends to avoid becoming homeless. We borrow to buy cars, which of course provide transportation to our jobs. So I acknowledge that borrowing is part of the American way that isn't going away. However, if you have to borrow, do so with caution and with the intention of getting rid of the debt as soon as possible.

There is an Old Testament story that provides a guideline for borrowing. An impoverished widow cried out to the prophet Elisha, asking for help to prevent her husband's creditors from taking her two sons as slaves to satisfy the unpaid debt. Here's what Elisha advised her to do: "Go around and ask all your neighbors for empty jars. Don't ask for just a few. Then go inside and shut the door behind you and your sons. Pour oil into all the jars, and as each is filled, put it to one side" (2 Kings 4:3 – 4).

So the widow borrowed the jars, and she followed the prophet's instructions. "When all the jars were full, she said to her son, 'Bring me another one.' But he replied, 'There is not a jar left.' Then the oil stopped flowing" (2 Kings 4:6).

Consider how this particular borrowing went down. The widow sought wise counsel. Because we know her husband "revered the Lord," we can assume she also knew to pray about her situation. She didn't compound the problem with unwise borrowing. Put in modern terms, Elisha doesn't tell her to go borrow more money to get out of her trouble. I don't imagine the prophet would have advised this woman to get a consolidation loan or to borrow against the equity in her home. Then, as it is now, it was not wise to use new debt to pay off old debt. Instead, the widow used borrowed jars and oil supernaturally provided by God to make some money. She used the borrowed assets — the jars — to create a stream of income to pay off her debts.

The story wraps up with Elisha telling the widow to "Go, sell the oil and pay your debts. You and your sons can live on what is left" (2 Kings 4:7). Notice he told her to pay off her debts *first*. He didn't say go invest the money. He didn't tell her to buy provisions for her and her sons. He told her to pay her debts and, with what's left, take care of their needs. I've often worked with people in debt who continue to spend on themselves while owing others. They take vacations, go to the movies, and eat out, all the while claiming they don't have enough money to pay down their debts. So their creditors have to wait to get their money while these borrowers indulge themselves first. This is just not right, and it's not biblical.

The widow's story provides an example of someone forced to borrow but who sought wise counsel about her situation, worked to get out of debt, and quickly repaid what she owed. This story is a blueprint for wise borrowing.

PAY OFF YOUR MORTGAGE

I'm amazed when people ask me if they should pay off their mortgage early. Why wouldn't you want to get rid of the largest debt you have as soon as you can? They probably ask the question because they've heard some financial experts say it's better to keep the mortgage debt and take any extra cash they would have used to pay the mortgage down and invest it instead.

But guess what? Most people don't invest their money. They spend it.

One thing I remember about my grandmother, Big Mama, is her obsession with paying off her mortgage before she retired. Taking a mortgage into retirement doesn't carry the same stigma it once did, according to one survey by Bell Investment Advisors. The survey found that many baby boomers — people born between 1946 and 1964 — are in no rush to pay off their mortgages.

Big Mama would have thought these people were nuts. This idea of keeping a mortgage years, or even decades, into one's retirement is completely opposite from what my grandmother, a child of the Great Depression, taught me. She always preached that I should pay off my mortgage before I retire to get rid of the most significant expense in my budget. There was a time when people would throw parties to celebrate being released from the bondage of a mortgage.

Yet another reason people convince themselves that it's smart to hold onto a mortgage is so they can deduct the interest payments. This argument drives me crazy. Here's an illustration to explain why keeping a home loan for the tax deduction is crazy.

To keep things simple, let's say you spend $1 in mortgage interest annually, and you're in the 35 percent tax bracket. Simply put, you *spend* a buck to get 35 cents back from the federal government.

But what if you kept your dollar (meaning you had no mortgage and thus no interest payments)? Yes, you may have to pay 35 cents in income taxes, but you get to *keep* 65 cents because you have no mortgage or interest payments. So, which would you rather have — 65 cents of your own money, or 35 cents that the government returned to you? In other words, why would you pay a lender $1 to get back 35 cents, when you could keep 65 cents even after paying 35 cents in taxes?

Now if you must have a tax deduction, there are other ways to get a tax break. To continue with the example above, instead of paying $1 in mortgage interest to a mortgage lender, you can give that same dollar to the church or to a charity, and the government will still give you back 35 cents.

Keep in mind, a mortgage payment is front-loaded with interest; for the first ten years a relatively small amount of each mortgage payment actually goes to paying off the principal. As the years go by, your interest-related tax deduction will decrease substantially anyway. The wisdom of my grandmother's generation about mortgages was right. They understood the risks. If you pay off your mortgage before you retire, you have more financial flexibility. You have a better chance to withstand a major illness or injury, a downturn in the economy, or a drop in the stock market.

Of course you need to save and invest too and not just put all your money into your home. You are house rich and cash poor if you do that. That's not an ideal situation. You don't want to be in the position of having all your money tied up in your home. You'd have to sell the home or borrow against it if you needed cash.

If you decide to prepay your home loan, check with your lender to make sure there are no prepayment penalties. Most importantly, don't forget to specify that any extra mortgage payments are being applied correctly. Check your mortgage statement each month to make sure the payments have been applied to your principal.

Before you begin making extra payments on your mortgage, consider the following:

- Make sure you have an emergency fund as well as a "life happens" fund, which we discussed on Day 8, "The Salvation of Saving." You should have at the very least three to six months of living expenses saved in your emergency fund. You may need to save more if you work in an industry susceptible to layoffs. Keep in mind that if you lose your job and your income drops, you may not be able to tap into your home equity by getting a loan.

- If you have other consumer debt, such as credit card debt or student loans, pay them off first.

- Save for retirement. Once you begin making regular payments to a tax-advantaged retirement account, then you can begin paying down your mortgage.

- If you have children, you should save for their college education so that they don't have to borrow.

Finally, if people criticize you about paying off your mortgage, let me give you some help in defending your position. Here's a question I received from a reader participating in an online discussion on the *Washington Post*'s website: "People always tell me to hang on to the mortgage, arguing the merits of tax deductions, earning interest on the money that's freed up, etc. None of that moves me, but instead of launching into a detailed explanation about why being debt-free is preferable, I'd rather have a short, succinct comeback. How should I respond?"

I had an easy retort for this reader: Tell people you don't like being a slave.

DUCKING YOUR DEBTS IS WICKED

Do you screen your calls in order to avoid your creditors? Or do you have your children lie for you when a creditor calls? When you get extra money, are you paying your debts first? Listen to what the Bible says: "The wicked borrow and do not repay, but the righteous give generously" (Ps. 37:21). Also, "It is better not to make a vow than to make one and not fulfill it" (Eccl. 5:5).

I can understand if circumstances have made it difficult for you to honor your debts. This is especially true when the economy is in a mudslide. Many people experience job losses or don't have suffi-cient funds to compensate for rising consumer prices. However, you should make every effort to pay back what you owe as soon as you are able. It's the moral thing to do.

When you can't pay your debts, one thing you should not do is let the phone keep ringing or let it go to voicemail when a creditor calls. Even if you don't have the money to pay the debt, be honorable and let the collection agency or attorney know your circumstances. Don't duck your creditors. Don't be afraid to pick up the phone. US federal law provides protection from unscrupulous debt collectors. Here are some of your rights based on the Fair Debt Collection Practices Act:

- You don't have to tolerate harassment. The creditor can't use profanity or threaten harm to you or your reputation.

- You don't have to endure an onslaught of harassing telephone calls at ungodly times. Generally that means creditors can't call before 8 a.m. or after 9 p.m.

- You don't have to put up with calls at your job. Debt collectors can't call you at work if you tell them that your employer disapproves.

- You can stop creditor calls by writing a letter to the collection agency telling it to cease calling. However, the creditor is permitted to contact you again to inform you of a specific action that it plans to take. A word of caution: Sending this letter doesn't mean you don't have to pay what you owe. You can still be sued.

- You have the right to keep your debt problems private. A debt collector cannot contact your friends, relatives, employer, or others except to find out where you live and work. If they do call someone looking for you, they can't tell the person you owe money.

These rules are intended to ensure you are treated with respect. Likewise, you should treat your creditor with respect. After all, if you owe the money, the company has a right to collect. So answer the telephone when the creditor calls. There is nothing more frustrating than trying to hunt someone down who owes you money.

I once had a renter in a condominium I owned. She was a single mother with a young daughter. She often had trouble paying her rent.

On multiple occasions I allowed her time to make up past-due rent amounts, without even charging a late fee. But as economic times for her got worse, she stopped answering my telephone calls when the rent was late. I would have continued to grant her grace had she only kept me informed of her situation. Finally, after not hearing from her for a few months, I had to begin eviction proceedings. Without a fuss, she packed up and left, never making even the slightest attempt to pay any part of the money she owed me.

In many cases, a creditor will negotiate with you to settle the debt for less than you owe. The key in such cases is to have some cash. If you can offer a lump-sum cash offer, you're more likely to obtain a reasonable settlement. From the creditor's perspective — and I know because I've been there — a promise to pay something *today* is much better than a vow to pay something in the *future*.

For example, let's say you have an old debt that has ballooned to $5,000 with fees and interest. It's not likely the creditor is going to accept an offer for you to pay $10 a month. However, if you can scrimp, save, and sell enough stuff to come up with a $1,500 lump sum, you have a better chance for a settlement.

Avoid being pressured to pay an amount you can't afford. It's important to agree to a payment plan that you can really follow to the end. You've already broken your word once, so don't put yourself in a position to do it again. There's no point in promising money you won't have. This will only further frustrate the debt collector and stress you out too.

The amount of a lump-sum cash offer that a creditor will accept can vary greatly. Generally, each state sets a statute of limitations on when a debt collector can sue to collect on an old debt. However, even if you can't be sued, the debt collector still has the right to collect your past-due debt.

Be sure to get the details of any debt settlement in writing before you send money to the collection agency or attorney. After you've settled the debt, keep a record of everything, forever! Because old debts are sold and resold, it's possible the proof that you paid your debt may not get transferred to the next agency trying to collect on old debts. Years after you've settled the debt, you might start getting calls from a new collection agency.

IS FILING FOR BANKRUPTCY EVER OKAY?

If at all possible, avoid filing for bankruptcy. You should do everything in your power to pay what you owe. But the reality is that people have hardships. One of the top reasons people file for bankruptcy is not because of credit card debt or because they chose to live high and pay later. It's because somebody in their household is sick and has overwhelming medical bills.

Nearly half of all Americans who file for bankruptcy do so because of medical expenses, according to a study by researchers at Harvard Law School and Harvard Medical School. This study helps put to rest the notion that most people who file for bankruptcy are deadbeats trying to beat out their creditors.

If you're considering filing for bankruptcy, pray about it. Ask God, if it is in his will, to help you find a way to honor your word and pay your debts as promised. After all, you benefitted from the services or goods you purchased. Is it not moral or fair to figure out a way to pay back what you borrowed?

Many people file for bankruptcy unnecessarily and too quickly when faced with a financial hardship. With help from a professional credit counselor, you may be able to renegotiate with your creditors to pay off your debts or settle your medical bills without filing for bankruptcy. If you need help with your debts, go to *www.debtadvice.org* or call 1-800-388-2227 to speak with a credit counselor.

The key to avoiding bankruptcy is cutting your expenses, increasing your income, or both. You should not file for bankruptcy until you have exhausted all avenues to satisfy your financial obligations.

I believe Scripture allows for mercy in this respect. Our debts, like our sins, can be forgiven. In a parable, Jesus gives an example of mercy toward debtors: "Two people owed money to a certain moneylender. One owed him five hundred denarii, and the other fifty. Neither of them had the money to pay him back, so he forgave the debts of both" (Luke 7:41 – 42). Don't read this and think I've given you permission or even biblical evidence that bankruptcy is okay. It's not okay. I want to be crystal clear about this. You will be going back on your vow to pay your debts. As Ralph Waldo Emerson said, "Pay every debt, as if God wrote the bill!"

THE DEBT DASH PLAN

There are a number of ways to pay down your debt, but I've found one way in particular that has successfully helped people keep on track. I call it the "Debt Dash Plan," or DDP. On this plan, your effort to pay down debt is like running a 100-meter dash. The reigning 100-meter Olympic champion is often referred to as the fastest man or woman in the world. The 100-meter dash is a quick race. That's the concept behind the Debt Dash Plan. I want to show you how to jumpstart your debt reduction by paying off some debt quickly.

People on debt reduction plans often fail because they don't feel like they're making progress right away, so they give up. The key to the DDP is to pay off your lowest debt first. Getting rid of that debt fast — like a runner in the 100-meter dash — gives you a quick rush and motivates you to stay the course and tackle your other debts.

With this strategy you ignore interest rates. You list your debts starting with the lowest balance. Then you take the extra money you make from cutting your expenses, a second job, or both, and apply it to that debt, while making just the minimum payments on the other debts. When you've paid off the first debt, apply the full payment amount from the first debt to the one with the next lowest balance until that one is paid off. Continue with the third debt, and so on. By attacking the lowest-balance debt first, you'll be able to pay off smaller bills in just a matter of months. That, in turn, can motivate you to aggressively cut back your expenses and find more cash to throw at your debts.

Here's how you get started on the Debt Dash Plan:

- Pray. Ask God to forgive you for your past mistakes with his money.

- Forgive yourself. Things happen. You've made mistakes and now you're trying to make up for them. If you've been beating yourself up, stop!

- Gather up all your bills, credit card statements, and so on. You can't turn things around if you continue to ignore what you owe.

- List all your debts starting with the one carrying the lowest balance. Remember, the order in which you list the debts is determined by how much you owe, not the interest rate charged. However, if two debts are about the same, the debt carrying the higher interest rate is listed first.

- Identify any extra cash you can make by cutting your expenses, getting another job, or both. Use it all to pay down the debt with the lowest balance. Be sure that you inform the lender that the extra payments are to be put toward the principal and not counted as an extra payment. In fact, you might want to write a separate check or send the money separate from your regular payment. Pay only the minimum amount due on all the other debts. Once you've paid off the debt at the top of the list, take your extra money every month and apply it to the next debt on your list. Again, you're sticking with paying lowest to highest.

- Follow this regimen until all your debts are paid off. If you have extra money above what you've been saving, such as a tax refund or bonus, put it toward your Debt Dash Plan.

Here is an example of what a Debt Dash Plan looks like when you're just starting out.

DEBT DASH PLAN
Example #1

Creditor	Total Balance Owed	Minimum Monthly Payment Due	Interest Rate	Debt Dash Extra Payment
1. Credit Card #1	$1,000	$20	8.99%	$200 Total Extra Payment: $200 + $20 you were already making = **$220**
2. Student Loan	$3,800	$50	6.8%	———
3. Credit Card #2	$5,500	$110	16.9%	———
4. Auto Loan	$11,000	$258.34	6%	———

As you can see, the debts are listed from the lowest to the highest balance. Generally you do not include your home mortgage in this plan. You can, however, include a car loan and student loans.

This chart on the following page shows what the DDP looks like after you've paid off your first debt.

Now that the first credit card is paid off, apply the payment from the first debt to the debt with the next lowest balance.

Some criticize this method of debt reduction because they say you can save more money by paying off the debts with the higher interest rates first. These people ignore the fact that much of the reason people are in financial trouble is psychological. Paying off the highest-interest debt first makes sense mathematically; however, people in debt often get discouraged and abandon their payoff plan when the list of debts remains the same for too long. They become dispirited because they don't see any progress.

Again, the Debt Dash Plan can give you a psychological boost and help you achieve your goals. In my one-on-one work with couples and individuals, I've found that they get charged up when they're able to quickly cross off a debt from their list. They speed up their efforts to get out of debt. The result is they pay less interest than they would pay on the debts carrying the higher interest rates.

DEBT DASH PLAN
Example #2

Creditor	Total Balance Owed	Minimum Monthly Payment Due	Interest Rate	Debt Dash Extra Payment
1. Credit Card #1	$0	$0	8.99%	PAID OFF
2. Student Loan	$3,800	$50	6.8%	$270 (You are now applying all the money that went to Credit Card #1, including the $20 minimum payment). Total Extra Payment: $220 + $50 you were already making = **$270**
3. Credit Card #2	$5,500	$110 (Keep making the minimum payment).	16.9%	——
4. Auto Loan	$11,000	$258.34 (Keep making the regular monthly payment).	6%	——

As you end this day of the fast, resolve to follow the Debt Dash Plan to eliminate your debts. If you don't think you can do it on your own, contact the organization I listed earlier in the chapter (*www.debtadvice.org*). Most importantly, make a commitment to keep your debts to a minimum. And remember that avoiding debt isn't about living in fear. It's about trusting that God will provide.

DAILY ASSIGNMENT

If you have debt, make a commitment today to list every creditor, bank, relative, or friend you owe money to. The information on this list should be transferred to your Debt Dash Plan. Total the debt. This is an important exercise so that you can see just how much debt you've accumulated.

Take some time to reflect on your use of debt. In your journal, answer the following questions:

Has being in debt led you to do some things you know are wrong? If so, list them.

How has debt affected your life overall? For example, have you had to delay buying a home because you have massive credit card debt? Are you stressed when the mail arrives or the phone rings because of the creditor calls?

Is your debt burden weighing down your spirit? If so, how do you imagine life would be different if you were debt free?

The Curse of Credit

9 Days to Go: Credit Crush

Main Point: Credit is dangerous.

My Pledge: I will review my credit card statements going back at least three months and examine my spending on my credit and debit cards.

Credit is evil.

Yes, that's right. I said it. And I've been saying it for years. Each time I make that statement someone laughs. I suppose they laugh because they think I'm being absurd.

But am I?

This plastic payment instrument was introduced in the 1950s initially for diners to pay for their meals. Today it lives up to the definitions for *evil* listed in the Merriam-Webster online dictionary.

> **Evil**
> 1. morally reprehensible
> 2. inferior
> 3. causing harm

Evil, by definition, is a force that brings about harmful or unpleasant effects. In Old English, *evil* is translated as "exceeding due limits."

For many cardholders that's literally what has happened. They have exceeded due limits, going beyond the financial confines that paying cash imposes. For them, credit has become a curse.

TESTIMONY TIME: *Day 13*

I was allowing commercials to push me into spending money on clothes mainly because I thought that I had to have them to uphold an image. I also realized that my mother and grandmother operated in the same way as far as spending because they felt they were entitled to it. I wasn't thinking for myself or relying on what the Lord was speaking to me.

I had to break that generational curse. I continued the fast and realized that I had a little bit more money left over in the month. I also was able to rest better during that month because I practiced saying no to my friends and family about spending unnecessarily. They are still spending and have mounds of things, but I'm not. I only spend when I truly need something.

Min. Michele

The way many people use credit cards reminds me of the gamblers I saw during a visit to Las Vegas. When you walk through the casinos, you hear people shrieking as their slot machines pay off or after they have a lucky roll at the craps table. You may see the occasional blackjack player sitting in front of tall stacks of chips representing winning bets. People *seem* happy. They seem as if they have things under control. So having witnessed this scene, you convince yourself that if they can play and win, so can you.

But don't be fooled by the lights, sounds, and shrieking of winning gamblers. In the crowd, there are a lot more losers than winners. The same can be said about credit card users. There are a lot of losers who have fallen into the credit card trap, racking up thousands of dollars in debt.

Why do you think casinos allow customers to play with chips instead of cash? I suspect they know if people gambled with paper money, they wouldn't bet as much. Playing with chips — like using a credit card — separates you from the feeling of using (and losing) real money. I know that the card itself is not inherently evil. *People* fall into temptation and misuse their credit. They're irresponsible with their cards, and credit card policies help make it easier for people to get into financial trouble.

In one survey conducted for LendingTree, an online company that connects borrowers with multiple loan offers, 50 percent of respondents confessed that they were concerned or extremely concerned about the amount of credit card debt they were carrying. Of those who expressed such concern, 10 percent had filed for bankruptcy, citing it as the only way to solve their debt problems. Here's something else noteworthy from that survey: Almost a quarter (22 percent) of respondents (people ages 35 to 54) had consolidated their card debt into one loan only to then accrue unmanageable credit card debt once again.

I frequently receive notes like this one from readers overcome with credit card debt:

> *I find myself in dire straits and do not know where to begin climbing out of the hole I have dug for myself. I went through a divorce several years ago and dealt with the emotional upheaval by maxing out all of my credit cards. After a few years, I could not make even the minimum payments on them.*

Scripture doesn't require that we stay completely away from worldly things. There are times when credit comes in handy. Let's say you purchased a computer online with a credit card, but it was never delivered. If you had paid for the computer with cash, you'd have to fight with the company on your own. However, under the federal Fair Credit Billing Act, if you have a problem with merchandise or services that you charged to a credit card, you have some protections.

The law requires the credit card issuer to investigate such consumer complaints. The issuer then has to take the charge off your bill or explain why it is correct. The investigation is required and must occur within two billing cycles and not later than ninety days after the issuer receives your complaint. In addition, you don't have to pay that portion of the credit card bill or related interest charges while the dispute is being investigated.

I hate this shallow Americanism which hopes to get rich by credit.

Ralph Waldo Emerson

Certainly there are times when credit is useful. However, more often than not, all credit does for you is allow you to live beyond your means. Some people are living the American Dream — on credit. But that dream can quickly turn into a nightmare when the accumulated debt gets out of control.

SO CAN YOU WIN AT THIS GAME?

The gambling analogy is particularly appropriate when it comes to credit. Even when you think you're winning, you're still losing money.

There are a number of academic studies that have found people spend more — even tip more at restaurants — when they use plastic. These studies show that even those of us who think we are using credit wisely are suckers.

I'll be honest. I spend more than I intend to when I pay with plastic. Although I don't carry a credit card balance, it's just easier to pick up that extra pair of pants or blouse or pair of shoes when I'm not limited to the cash I carry. The ease of using money interest free induces people to spend more. After all, spending cash for everything is also interest free. Some people smugly tell me they've beaten the banks at their own game because they don't pay any credit card interest. They get to use money for free, they boast.

However, even if they don't pay interest on the money because they settle the bill before the next billing cycle, or even if they collect a "free" plane ticket or two as part of a reward program, they're probably spending more than if they used cash. That means the banks win, and they lose.

Perhaps you're still not convinced.

"If I pay off all monthly credit card balances, why am I a sucker?" a cardholder asked me.

"I do not understand your argument that anyone who uses credit cards is a chump, even if they pay their balances off in full every month," another cardholder wrote. "I can assure you that I make the same purchases and contributions with credit cards that I would make without them."

I assure you, most people do not make the same purchases when they pay with plastic. This isn't just a feeling or based on anecdotal evidence. Researchers have found that people's willingness to purchase more products or services increases with the use of plastic.

In groundbreaking research, Drazen Prelec and Duncan Simester of the Sloan School of Management at MIT found that their study subjects paid more when instructed to use a credit card rather than cash. In fact, they found that people were willing to spend up to 100 percent more with plastic. The study, "Always Leave Home Without It," found that all things being equal, people's willingness to spend more money could be increased when they were told they could use a credit card.

Peter Tufano, a professor of financial management at Harvard Business School, has found in his research that transaction credit card users — those who pay their bills off every month and who are not overly indebted — can keep their credit card purchases under control. However, keeping the debts manageable is not the same thing as spending less.

Tests have shown that fast food customers spend 10 to 30 percent more when buying with a credit or debit card. One fast food chain found that the average transaction rose from $4.50 to $7.00, or 55.6 percent, when the chain began accepting credit cards.

All the academic research shows that using cash provides a visual cue that you're actually spending real money.

Federal regulators and Congress recognized that consumers

needed help in making the credit card game a bit fairer for card-holders. So tougher regulations have been put in place, including the Credit Card Accountability Responsibility and Disclosure Act of 2009. For example, in a change from past practice, credit card issuers are no longer able to charge a late fee if your statement isn't sent in a reasonable amount of time — at least twenty-one days — to allow you a chance to make your payment on time. Other changes to make the game a bit fairer:

- Issuers can't allocate customer payments in a way that repays debts with higher interest rates last. This rule affects people who have one credit card with balances that carry different interest rates.

- Mailed credit card payments received by 5 p.m. on the due date are considered on time. When mailed payments are not accepted, such as on weekends or holidays, creditors must consider your payment received on the next business day as being timely.

- Except under certain circumstances, creditors can't raise the interest rate on existing balances. In the past, issuers could for any reason change your interest rate. Now companies can't apply new and higher interest rates on balances incurred before a rate increase went into effect, unless a cardholder is more than sixty days late in making a minimum payment. Banks have to stick to the promised fixed rate they offer. Advertisements may refer to a rate as "fixed" only if a time period is specified for which the rate is fixed, and the rate can't be increased for any reason during that time. When you open a credit card account, banks must disclose all of the interest rates that apply. There's a prohibition on increases in those rates, except under certain circumstances.

- The downside of updated credit card rules is credit card issuers will be tougher on you if you don't make your payments on time. Here are some steps you can take to handle your credit card debt more wisely:

  - Automate your bill paying. Absent extenuating circumstances, you'd better believe the banks are going to stick to the rules and impose late fees whenever you falter. If you're sixty days behind on your payment, they'll pounce on the opportunity to raise your interest rate. And by the way, the banks will still be able to raise your rates on new purchases if your credit profile changes for the worse. To avoid getting hit with a late fee or a rate increase, automate your payments. If you have a phobia about using technology, get over it. It's not really that difficult. There's the initial set-up time, which includes entering all your information, but after that, all you have to do is download the information. Online banking allows you to set up a system that alerts you when your bills are due.

– Get serious about paying off outstanding balances. Make a habit of charging only what you can pay off in the following month. Don't hang onto debt figuring you'll be able to roll existing debt onto new cards with a zero percent interest rate or a low interest rate. Lenders are tougher on granting new credit so such offers will be harder to get. Because the 2010 regulations increase the chance that banks will actually have to honor those rates, fewer customers will get such deals.

These credit card rules may make the credit game fairer, but the best way to increase your odds of winning is to limit how much you play.

DEBTORS IN TRAINING

You probably know Proverbs 22:6, which says, "Start children off on the way they should go, and even when they are old they will not turn from it." This proverb has turned out to be true for many parents who are unconsciously training their children to be debtors.

I'm amazed, and dismayed, at how credit is being introduced to children at an earlier and earlier age. Giving a credit card to children, teens, and even college students is a bad idea. The reason I often hear for giving kids and young adults a credit card is so that they can learn the proper use of credit. They'll learn to manage their money better, people argue.

But whose money are they managing? It's not their money!

Can young adults, or even teens, handle credit well? Some can. But it's more likely that your child will do what many adults do — misuse and overuse the plastic devil. In a study called "Campus Credit Card Trap" by US PIRG, the Federation of State Public Interest Research Groups, the organization found that a significant number of college students have high balances, late fees, and delinquencies.

In another study young Americans had the second highest rate of bankruptcy among demographic groups, just after those aged 35 to 44, according to Demos, a public policy research and advocacy organization. The rate of bankruptcy filings among 25- to 34-year-olds indicates that this generation will be more likely to file bankruptcy as young adults than were young baby boomers at the same age.

In yet another study out of Ohio State University, researchers found that young adults take on more credit card debt than their elders and pay it off at a slower rate. "If what we found continues to hold true, we may have more elderly people with substantial financial problems in the future," said Lucia Dunn, coauthor of the study and professor of economics at Ohio State University. "Our projections are that the typical credit card holder among younger Americans who keeps a balance will die still in debt to credit card companies."

For years, lenders set up tables on college campuses offering free stuff to entice students into signing up for credit cards. The companies understood that if they got to these young people early, they were likely to capture them as customers for a long time. Thankfully legislation that went into effect in 2009 prohibits credit card companies from enticing students to sign up for credit by offering giveaways.

Don't let your kids be hoodwinked by the credit card industry. Their goal is to get your kid hooked on credit. Don't listen to these dealers of debt. They do not have your child's best interest at heart.

HOW DOES THE WORLD GET YOU TO IGNORE THE TRUE COST OF CREDIT?

The world gets you to ignore the cost of credit through distraction.

Look at these one-line credit enticements:

"Free gift for applying."

"Reward points"

"Buy now. Pay later."

"Instant approval."

"No payment for 18 months."

"Let your car be your credit."

"Need cash fast?"

Notice the theme behind all these credit pitches. You're not waiting on God to deliver what you need; instead you're waiting to see if your credit will be approved.

I've seen people waiting in the checkout line, silently praying their credit card is approved. Would God truly approve of that?

Not only are we distracted from the cost of credit, we're now made to think cash is an inconvenience.

Remember the credit card slogan "Life Takes Visa"? Visa aired a series of commercials in which people hustled through checkout lines at fast food restaurants and retail stores. They purchased what they wanted by merely waving or swiping their Visa credit or debit cards. When a customer pulled out cash, everything came to a screeching halt. The cash-paying customer got harsh looks from fellow shoppers. Even the cashier was disapproving.

In one commercial, the announcer says, "Don't let cash slow you down."

The series of commercials were funny, but the subliminal message wasn't. See how twisted the messages have become? The ads were diabolical. Cash doesn't slow you down. It liberates you from credit by confining you to what you can afford.

Think about it. Have you ever been in a checkout line when the customer in front of you pulls out her checkbook? You may have looked at the person disapprovingly. You may have even contemplated moving to another line. You may have thought to yourself, "How dare she hold things up by paying with a check?"

We've been baited and snared by the advertising for plastic. Look at these advertising slogans:

- American Express: "Don't Leave Home Without It."
- Visa: "It's Everywhere You Want To Be."
- MasterCard: "There are some things money can't buy. For everything else there's MasterCard."

The underlying message of all these slogans is that you can't live without credit. Sure, there are some people who can't even fathom leaving home without a credit card. It's their security blanket. But isn't God supposed to be our security blanket? Shouldn't we be putting our trust in him?

The overreliance on credit goes against biblical principles. Remember this verse: "Command those who are rich in this present world not to be arrogant nor to put their hope in wealth, which is so uncertain, but to put their hope in God, who richly provides us with everything for our enjoyment" (1 Tim. 6:17).

For everything else there isn't just MasterCard. On this day of the fast, remember that for *everything* there's God.

DAILY ASSIGNMENT

For today's assignment I want you to really think about your credit card purchases, even if you pay off the bill every month. Would you make these same purchases if you were limited to cash? One of the objectives of this fast is to break the hold credit has on you. On this day of the fast, write down in your journal the answers to these five questions:

1. *How has MasterCard (or Visa) become my master?*

2. *How would I buy the things I need, or want, if I couldn't use credit?*

3. *How has credit card debt impacted my marriage or other relationships?*

4. *How much more would I have in savings if I didn't have to make credit card payments every month?*

5. *How have I felt since I've had to stop using credit for the fast?*

Pull out your credit card statements for the last three months (leading up to the fast). Write down the total you spent for each month. Without looking at the itemized list of your purchases, try to remember what you bought. Why do this? Evidence shows that consumers often can't recall recent purchases bought on credit. If you can't recall what you purchased, isn't it likely you didn't need the items or service?

Cosigning Is Crazy

8 Days to Go: Cosigning Blues

Main Point: It is stupid to cosign.

My Pledge: I will not cosign with anyone other than my spouse. But if I decide to cosign for someone, I will make sure I can afford to pay the debt in full should the person default on the loan.

It's stupid to cosign.

Let me clarify that statement just a bit. It's stupid to cosign a loan for anyone other than your spouse.

I know calling someone *stupid* is not polite. In fact, in my house, *stupid* is considered a cuss word. But in this one particular case, I need to use the strongest word possible to convey not just what I know personally and professionally to be an unwise financial move, but what Scripture also calls senseless.

The word the Bible uses for cosigning is *surety*, meaning you become legally liable for the debt of another. So how does cosigning factor into your fast?

Part of the reason so many people can't prosper is because they act recklessly with the money God has entrusted to them. You can't achieve prosperity by making decisions that jeopardize your household wealth, which is what can happen when you cosign.

Matthew Henry's *Concise Commentary* says about cosigning, "A man ought never to be surety for more than he is able and willing to pay, and can afford to pay, without wronging his family."

When you cosign, you're being asked to take a risk that the lender didn't want to take. If the person was a good risk, then the lender wouldn't need a commitment from a backup borrower.

The strongest warnings about surety or cosigning can be found in the book of Proverbs. Here are four such warnings:

> Whoever puts up security for a stranger will surely suffer, but whoever refuses to shake hands in pledge is safe. (Prov. 11:15)

> A man devoid of understanding shakes hands in a pledge, and becomes surety for his friend. (Prov. 17:18 NKJV)

> Do not be one who shakes hands in pledge or puts up security for debts; if you lack the means to pay, your very bed will be snatched from under you. (Prov. 22:26–27)

> Take the garment of one who puts up security for a stranger; hold it in pledge if it is done for an outsider. (Prov. 27:13)

Now, you may be thinking that you're not dumb enough to cosign for a stranger. But surely it's okay to cosign for a neighbor, friend, or relative, right?

Let's look at this question by examining what Solomon says in Proverbs 6:1–5:

> My son, if you have put up security for your neighbor,
>   if you have shaken hands in pledge for a stranger,
> you have been trapped by what you said,
>   ensnared by the words of your mouth.
> So do this, my son, to free yourself,
>   since you have fallen into your neighbor's hands:
> Go — to the point of exhaustion —
>   and give your neighbor no rest!
> Allow no sleep to your eyes,
>   no slumber to your eyelids.

Free yourself, like a gazelle from the hand of the hunter,
    like a bird from the snare of the fowler.

Solomon taught this lesson to his son. My grandmother, Big Mama, taught it to me. Big Mama didn't like borrowing anything from anyone, and she definitely didn't loan people money.

Therefore I say to you never involve yourself in debt, and become no man's surety.

Andrew Jackson

Big Mama was particularly persnickety about cosigning. She considered cosigning to be lending someone your good name. My grandmother said she worked too hard and too long to just give away her good credit or be taken down financially because some triflin' person didn't pay back a loan she cosigned for. As a result, Big Mama never cosigned for a soul, not even me, and I had always been a good steward of my money.

I used to think Big Mama was being selfish by refusing to cosign even for close family members in need of a loan. I didn't understand what the big deal was. In fact, I was livid when she refused to cosign a car loan for me after I graduated from college.

When I went to the dealership for a loan, I was turned down because I didn't have a credit history. The dealer said I could get the loan if I found a cosigner. Not realizing what was in store for me, I asked my grandmother to cosign. I gave my grandmother the loan papers, thinking she would definitely sign since I had a full-time job working at the local newspaper. I was living with her at the time. I was her Mini-Me. I was as frugal as she was. It wasn't even a large loan, just about $5,000 for a four-door Ford Escort. I didn't think it was an unreasonable request. I didn't go for any bells or whistles. The car didn't even have air conditioning. But the tongue lashing that came after my request is one I'll never forget.

"Have you lost your everlasting mind?" Big Mama screeched.

She didn't quote a single Scripture, but nonetheless the message was the same as Solomon's in Proverbs.

"If the bank, which has much more money than I do, doesn't think you are able to handle the loan, then what makes you think I can handle it if you don't pay it like you're supposed to?" Big Mama said.

I was heartbroken to think my grandmother didn't trust me. I cried. But my tears had no effect on Big Mama. She told me to "hump it up the hill" and ride the bus until I could qualify for the loan on my own. And that's exactly what I did. It took about six months before I could qualify for the car loan on my own.

WHY COSIGNING IS STUPID

Cosigning is the worst form of debt.

If you stop for a moment and really think about what you're doing, you'd have to agree that cosigning is crazy. Here's something people don't fully comprehend with cosigning: You are pledging to pay a debt for an asset that you have no control over. You are signing up to pay for something for which you get no return, nor do you have any control over how the debt is being repaid. You have all the downside of the debt and no upside.

Even if the primary borrower pays the loan on time, it can affect your ability to borrow because as long as the loan is outstanding, it's the same as if you owed the money. That means the amount you can borrow is limited for as long as you remain a cosigner.

I want to make sure you truly understand what cosigning means. Take a look at the characteristics of cosigning.

The Loan (Auto, home, boat, etc.)	Primary Borrower (The one asking you to cosign)	Cosigner (You)
Typically has ownership interest in the asset	YES	NO
Responsible if payments are not made on time	YES	YES
Credit history is damaged if late or no payments made	YES	YES
Creditor can pursue and file a lawsuit for late fees and attorney fees if loan goes into default	YES	YES
Creditor may get a wage garnishment for the unpaid debt	YES	YES

The Federal Trade Commission says studies of certain types of lenders show that for cosigned loans that go into default, as many as three out of four cosigners are asked to repay the loan.

That certainly was the situation faced by one grandfather who wrote to me. The man's granddaughter had been going to college for about three years, got very sick with clinical depression, and dropped out of school. After receiving medical treatment and medication, she attempted to go back to school only to drop out once again.

"Currently she does not seem to be motivated to get back into college to finish up her degree," the grandfather wrote. "She has about five loans out for almost $100,000."

The grandfather had cosigned one of the loans worth $25,000. The granddaughter failed to pay the loan cosigned by her grandfather, so it had increased to $35,000 with interest and late fees.

"I am sure all the other cosigners, who are relatives, have had their loans inflate too," the desperate grandfather said. "What can we do to get this large expense off our backs? We are tired of talking to bill collectors. Our hard-earned credit is going down the drain!"

He signed the note: "A grandpa who is about ready to disown his granddaughter."

Oh, how this grandfather, who was trying to do a good thing, wishes he could free himself, like a gazelle from the hand of the hunter.

MAKE HASTE TO GET OUT

Depending on your state, the lender can collect a debt from the cosigner without first trying to collect from the borrower. The creditor can also use the same collection methods against you that can be used against the borrower, such as suing you or garnishing your wages. If this debt is ever in default, that fact may become a part of your credit history.

If you have already cosigned for someone else, Solomon recommends getting out of the obligation as quickly as possible. Don't rest,

Solomon says, until you've freed yourself of this obligation. "Free yourself . . . like a bird from the snare of the fowler" (Prov. 6:5). That's good advice. However, it's nearly impossible to detangle yourself once you've pledged to pay for somebody else's debt.

Still, there may be two ways to get out from under this type of loan. You can:

1. Try to get the primary borrower to refinance the loan. Of course, the reason the person needed a cosigner was because the lender didn't think he or she was creditworthy in the first place. But if a few years have passed since the person first took out the loan, he or she may be in a better financial situation — better paying job, better credit history — to qualify for a new loan.

2. Pay the loan off yourself. That's what I told that grandfather whose granddaughter has defaulted on the $25,000 student loan. He's stuck and you may be too. If the primary borrower is consistently paying late, you may have no other choice but to pay off the loan to save your good credit.

There's a third way. You could appeal to the lender to release you from this obligation. However, I've never seen this work. And why would the lender agree to release you as a cosigner? From the lender's perspective, two people on the hook increases the chance the loan will be repaid.

DON'T GIVE ANYONE A PIGGYBACK RIDE

Have you heard the term *piggyback* before? Routinely, people in credit trouble are advised that one way to rebuild their credit is to get somebody — their mama, daddy, grandparent, or friend — to add them on a credit card as an authorized user.

This practice, called *piggybacking*, has become controversial because some people have "rented" their credit to strangers who are trying to improve their credit scores to qualify for a loan. There's no question the intent here is to mislead lenders.

Piggybacking is a great deal for the person trying to establish credit or get a boost to a badly bruised credit history. What generally happens is the credit history for that particular account is transferred to the credit report of the authorized user. Obviously, the point of doing this is to become the authorized user on an account that is in good standing. However, any and all account information — good and bad — can be added to the authorized user's credit files. Positive information, such as on-time payments, can significantly help the authorized user's credit scores.

Here's the danger with having an authorized user on your credit card. He or she has permission to use the card but no contractual responsibility to repay any of the charges, including any purchases they've made.

Although technically an authorized user isn't responsible to pay the card charges, some lenders attempt to collect from the person anyway. What happens far more often, though, is the primary cardholder gets stuck with paying charges made by an authorized user.

Here's what one woman wrote to me after she let someone piggyback on her credit card:

> I have a friend whom I added to my account as an authorized user. She transferred her debt from another credit card so that she could get zero percent for a year and pay it off. A year passed and she is not able to pay it.

In this case, the damage was relatively minor. This Good Samaritan got stuck paying her friend's relatively modest $2,800 in credit card debt. However, I've known other instances where the amount was considerably higher.

If you are determined to let someone piggyback on your card, at least heed the following advice:

- Lower the credit limit on the existing card or use a card with a low credit limit. The point is to limit your financial exposure should the authorized user bolt on you and leave you stuck with the debt.

- Authorize the person to use only an amount of the credit line that you can afford to pay yourself.

- Keep track of how the other person's credit rating is doing so you can remove him or her as an authorized user as soon as possible.

TESTIMONY TIME: *Day 14*

During the fast, my wife and I realized how much we spent unnecessarily and where we impulse spent. But the thing that helped us most was learning how we could accelerate paying off debt. We decided not only to pay the bills on time, but also to pay extra on the principal, taking one debt at a time and charting our progress. This fast was a good exercise, and we will use it from time to time to make sure that we are being good stewards of our finances.

Jaime

IF YOU'RE HARDHEADED

Consider yourself warned that Scripture highly discourages cosigning. But if you're determined to do it anyway, at least protect yourself. The Federal Trade Commission offers this guidance:

- Make sure the loan you sign today is a loan you can pay off tomorrow if the primary borrower defaults.

- Even if you're not asked to repay the debt, your liability for the loan may keep you from getting other credit because creditors will consider the cosigned loan one of your obligations. Before you pledge property to secure the loan, such as your car or furniture, make sure you understand the consequences. If the borrower defaults, you could lose these items.

- Ask the lender to calculate the amount of money you might owe. The lender isn't required to do this, but may do so if asked. You also may be able to negotiate the specific terms of your obligation. For example, you may want to limit your liability to the principal on the loan, and not include late charges, court costs, or attorneys' fees.

In this case, ask the lender to include a statement in the contract similar to: "The cosigner will be responsible only for the principal balance on this loan at the time of default."

- Ask the lender to agree, in writing, to notify you if the borrower misses a payment. That will give you time to deal with the problem or make back payments without having to repay the entire amount immediately. Make sure you get copies of all important papers, such as the loan contract, the Truth-in-Lending Disclosure Statement, and warranties — if you're cosigning for a purchase. You may need these documents if there's a dispute between the borrower and the seller. The lender is not required to give you these papers; you may have to get copies from the borrower.

- Check your state law for additional cosigner rights.

Of all the warnings about avoiding debt, cosigning is probably the most difficult to heed because it's about helping someone. You may want to help a friend or relative get a needed vehicle. You may want to help someone become a homeowner. People cosign for other people they care about or once cared about. The intentions behind cosigning are good. I understand that. However, the outcome of a cosigning deal gone bad can get very ugly. So, unless you are in the financial position to assume the debt of the person you are cosigning for without any animosity or damage to your own finances, don't cosign.

DAILY ASSIGNMENT

If you've cosigned and the person didn't pay and now you are harboring ill will, pray today for God to remove your anger. Find a way to forgive the person for hurting you financially. Scripture says, "If anyone takes what belongs to you, do not demand it back" (Luke 6:30).

Make a promise to yourself that if you are ever asked to cosign and you are intent on doing the deal, you will at least ensure that you could handle the payments or payoff should the primary borrower fail to pay.

Guard Against Greed

7 Days to Go: Greedily Ever After

 **Main Point:** Greed blocks your path to prosperity.

My Pledge: I will take an inventory of what I own so that I can guard against wanting more. I will be on the lookout for things that pull me in the direction of greed.

Greed blocks your path to prosperity.

On this day of the fast, consider how greed may have interfered with God's grace in your life.

Take your time with this question. The answer may not be as easy as you think because most people don't like to think of themselves as greedy. But greed is simply a desire to have more than you need. Jesus warns against greed and how it can drive a wedge between us and God. In the parable of the rich fool, Jesus tells the story of a man who had an abundant harvest, so much so that he built a bigger and better barn to store all his grain (Luke 12:16 – 21). He gave no thought to giving some away or how his abundance was a blessing. He didn't even thank God for what he had. He did what kids do when you break open a piñata. He scrambled to pile up his goodies.

Take some time right now to do a mental inventory of your home. In your mind, open up all the cabinets and closet doors. What do you see in your kitchen cabinets? I'll bet there is little, if any, room in those cabinets because you have so many dishes and so much cookware.

What's in the food pantry? Are you storing up supersized containers of food and household products? How often have you or your spouse or your children opened up the refrigerator or cabinets and declared, "There's nothing to eat in here," when in fact there was plenty of food in there?

> *Greed is a bottomless pit which exhausts the person in an endless effort to satisfy the need without ever reaching satisfaction.*
>
> Erich Fromm

Visualize what you have in your family room or your children's play area. Do your children have multiple storage bins overflowing with toys? And yet, on their birthdays or Christmas, you spend even more money to buy them more things to pile up in more bins. When you open a closet door, does stuff tumble down to the floor? Do you have a junk drawer? Now in your mind, go to your bedroom. Open up your closet. What's in there? Is there any room on the clothes rack? How many times have you had to replace the rod in your closet because it keeps buckling or breaking under the weight of so many items?

Don't forget to cruise through the closets down the hall where you've stuffed things that can't fit in your own bedroom closet. Yes, women, I'm talking to you. Do you have containers under your bed to store more shoes or clothes?

If you have a garage, where's your car parked? Is it in the driveway because your garage is filled with stuff?

We already have so much, yet we want more. Aren't we storing up an abundance of clothes, shoes, purses, suits, ties, baseball caps, jewelry, toys, DVDs, electronic equipment, kitchen gadgets (we rarely use), and food for more than a lifetime?

Our houses and apartments are stuffed with stuff. And just like the rich fool, many of us are building bigger homes to store our abundance! The average size of new single-family homes increased from

1,750 square feet in 1978 to 2,479 in 2007. Only after the 2007 recession hit did the size of new homes begin to decrease.

And because people have run out of space in their homes, many families now rent storage space. The self-storage industry has been one of the fastest-growing sectors of the commercial real estate industry over the last thirty years, according to the Self Storage Association. In 2007, nearly 1 in 10 US households rented a self-storage unit, an increase from 1 in 17 households in 1995. That's a 65 percent increase in 12 years. There is about 7.2 square feet of self-storage space for every man, woman, and child in the US.

Imagine that. We have so much stuff that we pay rent every month so that our stuff can have its own place to live!

TESTIMONY TIME: *Day 15*

The financial fast is a mixed blessing. It reminds me that I am blessed in that I typically don't spend a lot, but I am also blessed enough that I usually don't have to worry about spending.

The fast forced me to think more about unnecessary spending, and in my line of business—retirement consulting for institutions—it helped reinforce the message I needed to be providing to clients.

I purposely made no large purchases, did not use my credit or debit cards, and spent less on lunches. The key to having money to spend is being disciplined in your spending habits now so you have more money to spend on items that you need—not want—in the future.

Michael

GET RICH QUICK AND GO BROKE FAST

Did you know that worrying about not having enough actually makes you greedy, which in turn makes you more susceptible to get-rich-quick schemes? There's a long passage in Luke where Jesus talks about how God will provide. I wanted to quote it in its entirety because the message is so important for you to grasp:

> Then Jesus said to his disciples: "Therefore I tell you, do not worry about your life, what you will eat; or about your body, what you will wear. For life is more than food, and the body more than clothes. Consider the ravens: They do not sow or reap, they have no store-room or barn; yet God feeds them. And how much more valuable you are than birds! Who of you by worrying can add a single hour to your life? Since you cannot do this very little thing, why do you worry about the rest? Consider how the wild flowers grow. They do not labor or spin. Yet I tell you, not even Solomon in all his splendor was dressed like one of these. If that is how God clothes the grass of the field, which is here today, and tomorrow is thrown into the fire, how much more will he clothe you — you of little faith! And do not set your heart on what you will eat or drink; do not worry about it. For the pagan world runs after all such things, and your Father knows that you need them." (Luke 12:22 – 30)

Why do people fall for scams?

In a word: Worry.

In many cases, people become victims of get-rich-quick schemes because they are worrying about not having enough. When a recession hits, it becomes prime time for scams and bogus business opportunities. When the stock market goes from bull to bear, people get scared and worried and open themselves up to crooks who promise unbelievable returns on their investments.

With the ups and downs of the stock market, people become more vulnerable to fraud or, at the very least, open to putting their hard-earned money into inappropriate investments. You have to be leery of investment opportunities that guarantee you'll make money in a down market. Con artists are masterful at gaining your trust, in some cases even getting on their knees and praying with you to get you to fork over your hard-earned money.

In one particularly infamous case, a federal jury convicted a

Georgia preacher of stealing nearly $9 million from 1,600 small black churches across the country. The charismatic preacher was able to "create an aura of legitimacy," prosecutors said, because his victims were impressed with his abundance of things. The minister told the faithful (who then told their friends and relatives) that he was developing Christian resorts around the country and that for a fee of $3,000 the churches could be "members" of his company. In return, he promised them a return of $500,000. Instead, this con artist spent investor funds on private jets, cars, limousines, and gambling trips to Las Vegas. This thief was eventually sentenced to seventeen years in federal prison and ordered to pay $7.9 million in restitution to victims and more than $598,000 in restitution to the IRS.

While the church members and their pastors were certainly victims, they were still guilty of trusting a man and not God. Had they not been so impressed with what the preacher drove or owned, they probably would have discovered he was a fraud. They should have discovered that the securities he was selling were not registered. One minister testified during the trial that he invested $3,000 and was told he could expect $200,000 back in less than a month!

Do you see the folly of these people putting their faith in this con man? The victims of the scheme were not on guard against greed. If they had been, they would have known better than to expect mammoth returns in such a short period of time for such a relatively small up-front investment.

When it came to investing, these church members should have heeded the warnings of the apostle Paul: "Those who want to get rich fall into temptation and a trap and into many foolish and harmful desires that plunge people into ruin and destruction" (1 Tim. 6:9).

Perhaps the motives of the duped were altruistic, to enrich their churches. But the bottom-line focus was still on getting rich fast. That is not the godly way to become prosperous. The Bible teaches, "Dishonest money dwindles away, but whoever gathers money little by little makes it grow" (Prov. 13:11). It is through consistent investing month after month, year after year — little by little — that you can become prosperous.

Here are several get-rich-quick schemes to be on the lookout for:

- *Affinity fraud.* This is perhaps the most insidious form of fraud. It's how the Georgia minister was able to con his victims. In affinity fraud, con artists often use religion or ethnic status to gain people's trust — and their life savings.

- *High-yield investments.* Con artists promise investors high returns if they invest in "risk-free, guaranteed, high-yield instruments." Here's an investment truth you can bank on: There is no high-return investment that is also low risk, so if anyone ever offers you that kind of deal, run. It's a low-down, dirty lie. Furthermore, don't invest in something you don't understand. Learn about it before investing any of your money in it. Always check references with the appropriate state or local government agency, the state attorney general's office, or the Better Business Bureau. A link on the North American Securities Administrators Association website (*www.nasaa.org*) will give you all the information you need to contact your local securities regulator.

- *Ponzi schemes.* This is a tried-and-true con in which the money collected from later investors is used to pay "returns" to early investors. The con collapses when not enough investors can be recruited to keep paying those who got in early. To learn more about this, go to *www.sec.gov/answers/ponzi.htm.*

- *Businesses in a box.* Thousands of people fall victim every year to swindlers peddling a variety of money-making business opportunities, according to the North American Securities Administrators Association. Promises of financial independence through work-at-home scams, illegal multi-level marketing schemes, plus a variety of phony business opportunities and franchises are among the most prevalent tactics swindlers use to prey upon people trying to earn some extra income. Before signing up for a business opportunity, check out: *www.business.gov/guides/franchises.* The website is managed by the Small Business Administration in partnership with twenty-one other federal agencies. Also go to *www.ftc.gov* where you will find lots of cautionary information about bogus *and* legitimate small-business opportunities.

One of my personal money mantras is "Keep it simple." Keeping it simple can be the most sophisticated thing you do with your money. Don't fall for get-rich-quick schemes that quickly leave you broke. Instead, "Be still before the Lord and wait patiently for him; do not fret when people succeed in their ways, when they carry out their wicked schemes" (Ps. 37:7). In other words, don't chase wealth from the wicked. Don't let greed block your path to prosperity.

I wanted to spend some time on greed today because you prepare yourself to prosper by getting rid of those things that stand in your way. Greed has a way of entering your life and causing you to do stupid things. It leads you right into the hands of wicked people who are intent on taking your money. It causes you to cheat, steal, and lie. And you may justify some of these actions by arguing that you need the money.

Have you ever been to a funeral where the deceased hasn't been in the ground for even a day and relatives are greedily grabbing at what's left in the estate? Heed the warnings of Scripture: "What causes fights and quarrels among you? Don't they come from your desires that battle within you? You desire but do not have, so you kill. You covet but you cannot get what you want, so you quarrel and fight. You do not have because you do not ask God" (James 4:1 – 2).

Guard against greed if you want to prosper.

DAILY ASSIGNMENT

Think about at least two decisions you have made that could be traced to greed. For example, do you have a lottery ticket habit? Do you have a history of investing in get-rich-quick business schemes that have never paid off? Have you been the victim of fraud because you wanted to earn money fast?

If you realize that you have given into greed, add up how much it has cost you. For example, if you play the lottery, how much have you spent in the last year on this game of chance? Calculate the money you've lost on bad business ventures. Now think of things you could have used that money on (like paying off a debt).

Make a commitment today that you will not give in to greed. If you play the lottery, give it up. Resolve that you will not respond to any investment offer or business deal without doing the following:

Pray first.

Seek wise counsel. This means gathering information and counsel from someone not connected to the person trying to sell the product, service, or small business idea.

Check with state or federal authorities to determine if any unsolicited offer you are considering is legitimate.

The Caregiver Cliff

6 Days to Go: Don't Be Scared of the Long-Term Care Conversation

Main Point: Millions of US households contain someone caring for an older relative or friend.

My Pledge: I will take some time to learn about long-term care insurance and begin planning for any caregiving responsibilities that may fall to me.

I was at my father-in-law's bedside when he took his last breath.

He was eighty-three and dying from lung cancer. His doctor had estimated he might have up to a year to live, but soon after his diagnosis, we realized he'd have much less time.

I'll be honest, when my father-in-law first came to live with us, he was in a dark place. And his presence ushered darkness into my home. He was angry most of the time because he had to give up his independence and rely on others to help him even with the smallest tasks. He had trouble feeding himself. He couldn't go to the bathroom by himself. He needed help getting dressed. He had to get my husband to manage his money. He was also in a lot of pain.

It's so hard to stay pleasant when the person you are caring for is so negative. There were times I would stand at the door to the room where he was staying and pray for strength to go in. I became depressed. I became angry. But after getting some counseling and great advice from a minister, my pastor, and his wife, I found a way to break through my father-in-law's darkness.

No matter how negative he got, I would greet him with joy. Rather than ask him how he was doing — to which he would always just complain — I would start with asking him to name at least one good thing for the day — a praise. If he couldn't come up with something, I volunteered something praiseworthy. I also began to touch him gently on his arms, hands, or shoulder. The touching helped calm him down when he would get the most upset and belligerent, especially at night when the aide was trying to prepare him for bed. My husband and children did the same. And you know what? It worked. Our joy became infectious. He would still complain, but he began to tell jokes and laugh more.

And just as things got better with his spirit, we learned his body was failing and failing quickly. The year we thought we had with him soon turned into a matter of weeks. Every morning I was afraid that we would find that he had died during the night. A hospice nurse had warned us that we might not be present when he died. But I wanted to be there. I wanted him to have the comfort of knowing he was cared for to the very end.

Soon after my father-in-law went into hospice care at our home, I had to take a business trip. I wanted to cancel but since we didn't know when the end would come, I took the chance and left. It was a one-day trip, and I asked God to get me back home before he closed his eyes for the last time.

When I returned from my trip, I dropped my suitcase at the door and rushed to his bedroom. I wanted to change out of my road-trip clothes, but something kept me by his side. I couldn't leave his room.

He could only groan by then because he was in even more pain. He rarely opened his eyes during the final days of his life. But about an hour and a half after I arrived at his room, he opened his eyes, turned his head, and stared at me. The nursing assistant hurried to get my husband. And, together, the three of us stood by his bed as his breathing slowed. He didn't want any extraordinary measures taken to keep him alive. I whispered to him that it was okay for him to go. And he did.

I believe he had waited for me.

TESTIMONY TIME: *Day 16*

This was the first fast of its kind for me. And I am glad to have had the experience. I came face-to-face with my vulnerabilities and identified room for greater fiscal discipline on the road to financial freedom.

Mildred

SCARY CAREGIVER STATISTICS

For several months, a much shorter time than we had expected, my husband and I joined the estimated 65 million people who give their time and money every year to care for sick or disabled relatives, most of them elderly.

We were fortunate; my father-in-law had been a great saver so he had resources to pay for his care. But many families are hanging near a "caregiver cliff." They are taking time off from work, and thus risking their jobs, or tapping into their limited financial resources to provide care for one or both parents or an elderly relative.

Just look at these facts from various reports by the Family Caregiver Alliance, AARP, and National Family Caregivers Association:

The value of the services provided annually by unpaid family caregivers is estimated at $450 billion.

About 66 percent of family caregivers are women. More than 37 percent have children or grandchildren younger than eighteen living with them.

Nearly half of the caregivers in one survey performed medical and nursing tasks.

Family caregivers spend an average of twenty hours per week providing care; 13 percent provide forty hours of care a week or more.

By the time my father-in-law came to live with us, he needed care around the clock. He couldn't perform any activities of daily living such as feeding, bathing, or dressing himself. Even with two shifts of aides, there were gaps that had to be filled by my husband and me.

Seventy percent of caregivers who work say they have difficulties on their jobs because of their caregiving roles.

Forty-seven percent of caregivers who work say that paying for caregiving expenses has caused them to use up all or most of their savings.

The numbers paint a grim picture, I know.

Although there are also joys in caregiving, anyone who's done it will tell you it's a tough job, and it can be a strain on your finances. If you suspect you might be responsible for caring for an elderly relative, begin to prepare now as best you can. If you're already a caregiver and looking for help, go to *www.aarp.org/home-family/caregiving*.

According to federal government projections, 12 million older Americans will need long-term care by 2020. And when they need that care, they will realize that they and the caregivers they will have to lean on are woefully unprepared for the cost. Most people, like my father-in-law, will be cared for in their home or someone else's home. Family and friends are the sole caregivers for 70 percent of the elderly.

Are you preparing yourself for what it will take to care for your parent or elderly relative?

LOOK INTO LONG-TERM CARE INSURANCE

How will you pay for the long-term care you might need? Are you expecting Medicare to cover it?

If so, think again. Medicare generally does not pay for long-term care, which assists people with daily living activities such as dressing, bathing, and using the bathroom. Medicare helps pay for medically necessary skilled nursing or home health care, but only if you meet certain conditions. Medicaid, the state and federal government program, will pay for some long-term care services, but it's limited to people with low incomes and limited assets.

Long-term care insurance can cover the cost of nursing homes, assisted-living facilities, and in-home care. In most cases, the insurance will cover expenses for those who need assistance with such daily activities as eating, dressing, and bathing, or who have a severe cognitive impairment such as Alzheimer's disease.

This insurance isn't cheap. Depending on your age and the options you choose, yearly premiums vary from $1,000 to as much as $8,000. One consideration with this type of insurance: Do you have assets that you don't want to spend down should you need long-term nursing home care? If you are nearly broke now, you may not be able to afford this insurance and you would quickly qualify for state aid.

Before you buy, do some research. Start by going to the National Association of Insurance Commissioners website, *www.naic.org.* Click on the link for "Consumer Resources" and then go to "Long-Term Care Insurance." You should also order a free copy of NAIC's "A Shopper's Guide to Long-Term Care Insurance." Another source for information is *www.medicare.gov.* There you will find a "Long-Term Care Planning Tool."

Long-term care insurance coverage can vary widely. Some policies may cover only nursing home care. Others may include coverage for a whole range of services like care in an adult daycare center, assisted living, medical equipment, and formal and informal home care. Premiums for long-term care insurance also vary, depending on your age and health status when you buy the policy and how much coverage you want. Because insurance companies look at how healthy you are when writing your policy, the younger and healthier you are, the lower the premiums. But here's the thing: the younger you are when you get the insurance, the more years you'll be paying for it. If you buy it at age fifty, you might not need the insurance for another twenty or thirty or even forty years. So carefully consider the right time to buy, making sure you can afford the premiums.

TALK TO YOUR PARENTS

It's not an easy conversation, but you have to talk to your parents about their long-term care plans. My grandmother, who was a good financial steward, refused to tell me much about her affairs.

"My business ain't none of your business," Big Mama would say anytime I tried to ask her about her money. "You'll know everything you need to know when I die."

My grandmother died at age eighty-two and never needed long-term care, but if she had, it would have been a tough battle to help her. At least I tried.

Many potential caregivers don't make the effort to talk to their elderly parent or relative until a health crisis forces the issue. In fact, a poll conducted by Harris Interactive Inc. found that 46 percent of adults surveyed said they had not taken any action to plan for care or companionship for an elderly relative, even though they estimated the person would need care within a five-year period.

As I've been saying, the 21-day fast is about facing financial issues, and long-term care is a big one. It's one you can't ignore. But I know what you might be thinking. *What can I do if my parent won't talk to me?*

Don't stop trying.

It's especially vital to try and have the talk before your mom or dad or both begin suffering from diminishing cognitive abilities. Keep pressing the issues, particularly if you notice signs of deteriorating memory or diminished ability to manage their affairs.

If you encounter resistance, pull back a little and let your aging parents or relative know that you just want to help them, not control them. Tell them you want to help them prepare for a time when they might not be able to handle their business. Here are some issues to address if you can get them to talk:

Find out if they have a living will and medical power of attorney. These advance directives are legal documents that allow an aging parent to designate someone to make health care decisions and convey end-of-life wishes. The National Institutes of Health has a website, *www.MedlinePlus.com*, produced by the National Library of Medicine, where you can get some basic information about this type of paperwork. On the site, search for "Advanced directives."

Find out if they have any insurance policies, including long-term care insurance. When my father-in-law came to live with us, we got advice to look into the Aid and Attendance (A&A) Program through the Department of Veteran Affairs. The pension benefit can provide monthly financial assistance to help pay for long-term care help received at home, at a nursing home, or in an assisted-living facility. This is a benefit that isn't well-known but is of great help to many senior veterans and their spouses or surviving spouses. The veteran has to have been honorably discharged and served at least ninety days, with at least one day during officially declared wartime. You also have to meet certain medical and financial qualifications.

I found the most helpful materials about this program at *www.veteranaid.org*. You'll find an abundance of information with advice, resources, and links. Do your research, because the application process is complicated and time consuming. It can take months before an application is approved. But it's worth the effort. As of 2012, the A&A pension benefit provided up to $1,732 per month to a veteran, $1,113 per month to a surviving spouse, or $2,054 per month to a couple, according to *veteranaid.org*.

Explore all the possible living options. One thing I wish we had done was to build a bedroom on the main floor of our home. We had to move my father-in-law into a basement bedroom, but that meant he couldn't be on the main floor a lot because he had trouble climbing stairs. You may have to make some home modifications (to theirs or yours), so be prepared for that cost. Other living possibilities include an assisted-living facility, a senior daycare center, or a nursing home.

Try to get an accurate accounting of their monthly income, savings, investments, and other assets. You might save this topic for the last part of your talk if your parents are particularly private about their affairs. If you start talking about the money first, they may think that's all you are concerned about. You want to emphasize that you aren't trying to take control but rather are trying to help *them* keep control over how their assets are used to care for them.

Don't try to be a martyr by trying to do it all yourself. Get help from siblings and other relatives. I say that knowing that may be difficult if not impossible. Nothing brings out sibling rivalry and old wounds more than debating and then deciding who has to take care of mom and/or dad. And if you are typically the person the family leans on, you may have to accept — with some good therapy — that you are going to carry a lot of the caregiving burden.

AARP is a good place to find information about caregiving. The organization has a caregiving resource center with a wealth of information at *www.aarp.com*. There's a tool to find a care provider, as well as checklists and information to prepare you before your caregiving starts. They even have a free call center. I can't stress enough how important it is to read up on what you'll be doing or check out the resources if you're already providing care.

Find out what community support there is by contacting your local office of aging. You can find the contact information by going to *www.eldercare.gov*. If you have the financial resources, consider hiring a geriatric care manager, a professional who specializes in helping families who are caring for older relatives. To find more information about this service, contact the National Association of Professional Geriatric Care Managers or visit the organization's website at *www.caremanager.org*. This is a nonprofit organization that provides referrals to licensed professionals, primarily social workers and nurses, who work with families in need of assistance with caregiving. These managers can review financial, legal, and medical issues, and offer referrals to appropriate professionals. This service is particularly helpful for long-distance caregivers. The costs can range from $80 to $200 per hour, depending on where you live.

If your parent or relative is hesitant to talk, try to see things from his or her perspective. Offer a helping hand, rather than being heavy-handed in how you approach the issue. Your dad may be concerned about being taken advantage of. Or your mother might fear losing control. And the truth is, relatives can and do take advantage of seniors. Financial fraud of the elderly is a growing problem. More than seven million older Americans — one out of every five citizens over the age of sixty-five — have been victimized by a financial swindle, according to the Investor Protection Trust. When experts were asked about the top three financial abuses against seniors, the results showed that theft or diversion of funds or property by family members came first, followed by caregiver theft, and then financial scams by strangers.

You may want to avoid this caregiving conversation — but you can't afford to. Keep trying to have the talk because in all that you will have to do, it's vital to effective caregiving to get a complete picture of what's in place and what financial resources are available, if any, to take care of your relative.

DAILY ASSIGNMENT

This day's assignment has two parts.

Investigate when and whether long-term care insurance is right for you. Look for unbiased information. By unbiased, I mean the information isn't provided by an agent, business, or organization that will benefit from your choice. In other words, your research shouldn't be limited to a conversation with an insurance agent. Look for articles or reports from Consumer Reports, consumer groups, or news stories that list the pros and cons of buying long-term care insurance. Once you've done some background research, you can then seek the help of an insurance agent.

If you have elderly parents and haven't had a talk about their care, set aside some time to have the conversation. You don't have to do it today, but make a date to have the talk. Your parents may be reluctant to discuss their retirement preparation, including whether they have enough money should they need care. But if you're likely to be the one taking care of them, keep pushing the issue.

Part Four

FASTING FOR FINANCIAL PEACE

In all the years I've written for the *Washington Post* and counseled individuals and groups, I've learned one important fact: at the core, money problems are seldom about money. Issues we have with debt, credit, entitlement, covetousness, greed, and even extreme frugality stem from our not addressing our own past in order to figure out why we do what we do with our money.

In these closing chapters, we'll take a closer look at the benefits and blessings of being brave enough to deal with the demons that have plagued our finances. And I want to encourage you with more testimonies of people who have faced and overcome the same obstacles you may be facing.

In the pages to come, you'll discover that stressing about money doesn't make things better. We'll explore the fear of being poor — one of my own issues. And we'll address the topics of stewardship and restored relationships. On Day 21 we'll wrap things up by celebrating what I hope you've achieved during the fast. If you've done even a fraction of what I've asked you to do throughout the twenty-one days, you will be a changed person. You will see that you have not only reached the end of the fast, but you have begun a journey to financial freedom.

Perpetual Peace

Main Point: Trust that God will bring financial peace into your life.

My Pledge: I will identify at least one aspect of my finances and decide today to stop stressing about it.

Financial peace is priceless.

You can't buy the joy that comes with running your financial life in a way that keeps trouble at bay. You can't purchase the peace that comes with trusting that even when you are hit with a financial struggle, God will see you through. Jesus said, "Peace I leave with you; my peace I give you. I do not give to you as the world gives. Do not let your hearts be troubled and do not be afraid" (John 14:27). That's the kind of peace I'm talking about.

There was at least one time in my life I was especially grateful that God had taught me how to handle my money well. It brought me peace at one of the most dreadful times in my life. When my daughter Olivia was seven, for two months she was hospitalized in an isolation ward at Children's Hospital in Washington, DC. Olivia had developed a rare condition brought on by juvenile rheumatoid arthritis. Her illness resulted in cells known as macrophages attacking and destroying her red and white blood cells. Essentially, Olivia's immune system was attacking her own body. During her hospital stay, she had to take an incredible amount of medication — pills that could choke a horse, liquids that made her gag, and shots that turned her arms and legs black and blue. She had to take so much medication that she collapsed in tears at the sight of a nurse coming into her room. Sometimes it took an hour to get her to take all her medications.

One of the things for which I was most grateful during that time was the fact that both my husband and I were able to take sick leave and vacation time. We used up all our paid leave so we could be with our daughter. At one point we thought we might have to take time off without pay. And yet even if we had to take unpaid leave, we were not worried about having enough money to keep up with our expenses. We were able to be with our daughter in that hospital room around the clock while also taking care of our two younger children.

When I sat by Olivia's bed and watched her breathe through an oxygen mask and moan in her sleep from all the drugs she had to take, I couldn't help wondering how much more scared and stressed I would have been if we hadn't had savings. We didn't know we were saving for this specific crisis, but we knew one would come.

I watched as many parents had to leave their sick children and go back to their jobs because they couldn't afford to lose time at work. I didn't know their financial situations, but I felt sorry for them. I watched as they walked down the hospital hallway, glancing back toward the rooms where their children were fighting for their lives. My husband and I could spend what might have been the last days of my child's life with her, comforting her. You may never be able to save enough to weather the type of storm we went through, but I thank God at least for those two months we didn't have to be concerned about paying the bills.

TESTIMONY TIME: *Day 17*

I moved from stress to strength. Here are the goals that I have achieved:

- *Paid off a personal loan.*
- *Paid off a student loan.*
- *Paying all bills ahead of schedule.*
- *Avoiding unnecessary bills, such as speeding tickets and late charges.*
- *Tithing.*
- *Established emergency savings ($200 per month).*
- *Paid off mortgage quickly and comfortably.*
- *Paid off charge cards.*

Through this process I have learned many things. Although financial discipline is necessary, this is also a process that requires faith, prayer, good stewardship, commitment, and sacrifice. The devil will look for ways to make me falter and fail. Giving up cannot be an option.

Angela

YOU CAN'T TAKE FINANCIAL STRESS TO THE BANK

You are in the home stretch of the fast, just five days from finishing. I hope by now the financial fast has led you to the revelation that you can make do with less, and have more as a result. If you've grasped that concept, even if you still have debt to be paid off, even if you have a job that just barely gets you by, you can be at peace. Many of the people who have gone through the 21-day financial fast have told me they did it because they wanted to finally get rid of the stress of not having enough money. They wanted peace in their house, in their marriage, and in their lives. In response to an online survey by the American Psychological Association, adults said that money was the number-one source of stress in their lives.

Here's an example of how stress over finances can be conquered. Kim and her husband, Greg, took on the challenge of the fast and joined Prosperity Partners ministry after going through a rough time.

> *Money and time are the heaviest burdens of life, and ... the unhappiest of all mortals are those who have more of either than they know how to use.*
>
> Samuel Johnson

Two years after getting married and purchasing a home, Greg lost his six-figure job, and shortly after that he became ill. He was unable to work for two years. "Once he became well enough to work again, it was difficult for him to find employment at the salary level he had before," Kim said. "It was tough."

They went through their emergency savings in about seven months. They cashed out their workplace retirement plans to stay afloat. When that money was gone, they resorted to using credit cards to make up any monthly shortfalls.

"By the time we had reached our seventh year of marriage, we were in a constant struggle to make ends meet. We were faithful tithers, and we continued to be so. But as the financial manager of the house, it seemed that no matter how hard I tried, I could not get us back to where we once were."

Kim went on to say, "As you can imagine, this led to many disagreements and struggles within our marriage."

When they could no longer fix things themselves, together they did three key things. They turned to the Lord, they joined Prosperity Partners, and they took the 21-day financial fast. "Once we began to put the Lord and your advice into action, all kinds of amazing and wonderful things began to occur in our life."

The small business her husband started began to take off. She got a promotion. When they started the fast, they were $130,000 in debt with no savings. The couple is now debt free. They are great savers.

"I was so overwhelmed with our financial problems," Kim said. "I honestly feel that if I had not attended that first meeting, I would still be stumbling down the path of how to put my life and the life of my family back together financially."

Kim and her husband found financial peace. And that is priceless.

SUBMIT TO GOD

Whether you have little or much, the lesson for today is to not let your heart be troubled when it comes to your financial situation. Instead of fretting about your finances, take action to make things better and watch how God will prove his Word true. That's a lesson Job learned well.

If you know Job's story, you know he remained steadfast in his faith despite great trials and tribulations. At one point Job's friend Eliphaz argues that Job's suffering was brought on because he had done something wrong. Of course, we know that's not true. Still, part of what Eliphaz says to Job has merit: "Submit to God and be at peace with him; in this way prosperity will come to you" (Job 22:21).

Your financial life may be a wreck, but don't lose faith. This fast can help bring serenity back into your life. I can't promise you everything will be fine when it's over, but I know that you'll be closer to finding financial freedom. If you already handle your money well, then the fast should confirm what you already knew — that following God's financial roadmap for your life takes you straight to a place of peace.

DAILY ASSIGNMENT

Make a list of all your money worries. What are the financial issues that are robbing you of your peace? For example, your list may start with the following: "I worry I won't have enough money in retirement."

Pick one thing from your list and pray about it. Ask God to show you a way to experience tranquility regarding this issue.

After you pray, do some research to determine how you might resolve the concern you've chosen. For example, if your worry is having enough money in retirement, go online to www.choosetosave.org/ballpark/. On the website you will find the "Ballpark" retirement calculator. Use this tool to find out how much you need to save. Don't be intimidated by all the questions. It's worth the time it takes to complete the exercise to determine if you are saving enough. If you find you are way off from having enough, don't panic. Save what you can.

Broken Bonds

4 Days to Go: Better than Blessed

Main Point: It's okay to embrace your wealth.

My Pledge: I will stop worrying about not having enough money, because God has so richly blessed me.

Perhaps for you this fast was never about not having enough — money, savings, investments, or discipline. It was never about getting out of debt. Maybe for you it was about letting go. Perhaps the bond you needed to break was fear. You know you have an embarrassment of riches, and yet you still worry and fret over your finances.

Throughout this book I've told you about my grandmother, Big Mama. She was a savings guru. How this woman was able to set aside so much of her meager paycheck every week has been an inspiration to me my entire life. In many respects it was her financial lessons that led me to create the 21-day financial fast.

Big Mama was great at teaching me how to save. What she didn't do well was show me how to spend and not feel guilty about it. For most of my life, the bond I've had to break was the fear of not having enough.

Fear and I were buddies, hanging out on most days. I was so yoked with the fear of poverty that I couldn't rejoice in the prosperity God

213

had delivered to me. I don't think Big Mama ever felt comfortable spending money, even when she purchased something she had saved up for. Unfortunately, I'm just like her in that way. Call me well-off and I'm liable to slap you.

I know I'm not alone. In one study, Visa found that an increasing number of affluent individuals, people age 35 to 54 whose household incomes were at least $125,000 per year, reported embarrassment with being identified with wealth and status. Although their household income was at least triple the national median, more than a third (39 percent) of these affluent individuals described themselves as "middle class," while a little more than half (52 percent) thought of themselves as "upper middle class." Seventy-two percent said they didn't like, or were embarrassed by, the terms "wealthy" or "well-off" to describe their economic situation.

When my husband and I built our home, for the longest time I was embarrassed to tell people where I lived. I was ashamed that I could afford such a nice home. I was raised to believe you should always handle your money as if you were one shopping spree or paycheck away from being poor. The way I've lived my life is described perfectly in the Scripture that says, "One person pretends to be rich, yet has nothing; another pretends to be poor, yet has great wealth" (Prov. 13:7). I epitomized the latter. I played poor for a long time. What I had to learn was to accept and appreciate God's favor and give up the fear of abundance.

EMBRACE YOUR PROSPERITY

At some point we lifelong savers have to learn that living well isn't a sin. If you're doing all the right things — tithing, working hard, living below your means, saving for your retirement, giving to charitable causes, and putting away money for your child's college education — then it's okay to splurge sometimes.

You certainly don't want to boast about your wealth, but you shouldn't be embarrassed by it either. You should not worry about losing it. Meditate on this Scripture: "When times are good, be happy" (Eccl. 7:14). Even if you lose your wealth, God will still provide. Ecclesiastes 7:14 continues, "But when times are bad, consider this: God has made the one as well as the other."

Sometimes you have to let go of your money. If you've made wise decisions and you're financially secure, then go ahead and spend a little. Splurge on yourself or a loved one. Don't wait until you're darn near death to enjoy some of what God has blessed you with.

I often hear from readers of my newspaper column who just can't get their spouses or relatives to splurge even though they've managed their money well. Or I hear from readers who are nervous about spending money they've saved, especially during a recession or terrible economic downturn.

For example, I received this question from a reader: "I am going to buy my first car in twenty-five years, since my 1981 Camaro is ready to be put out to pasture. The car I want is about $50,000. I have the cash, but I could finance it through the bank or the dealer or I could get a home equity loan. Which option is best? If I pay cash, I will pay my savings back monthly at the same rate at which I would pay off a loan."

My first instinct was to yell at anyone spending $50,000 for a car. Who needs a $50,000 car? Nobody *needs* a $50,000 car. And yet if you can truly afford it — and it's what you want — why shouldn't you buy it? I wouldn't finance that much car if I had the cash (and even if I didn't have the cash). Still, if you have cash like that and you're generous and a good steward over your money, then treat yourself. You can't take it with you.

BREAK YOUR BOND

By this point in the fast I hope you've identified the financial bond or bonds you need to break. In this chapter I've concentrated on just one. It's an issue that many think they would love to have. What they might not know is that it can be just as troubling to live in a household with a person who has money but is always worried about losing it. This person is like the seed that falls among the thorns, which Jesus said, "stands for those who hear, but as they go on their way they are choked by life's worries, riches and pleasures, and they do not mature" (Luke 8:14).

If being guilty about being well-off is not your issue, think about what bonds *are* keeping you in financial bondage. Use today's teaching to dig deep and to figure out why you shop too much or spend too much or can't be happy with what God has blessed you with. Get counseling if you have to, but address your issues. Otherwise you won't conquer the bonds that bind and keep you from having financial peace.

TESTIMONY TIME: *Day 18*

As a forty-something professional who was fairly successful and happy in most areas of my life, I nevertheless had difficulties managing my finances. The fast was not something I wanted to do—it was something I had to do!

I thought it was going to be too difficult for me to commit to not spending. I love fast food and Starbucks, but I realized they were not necessities. It was my wants—not my needs—that I had to set aside for twenty-one days. Although I had to plead my case with Michelle to maintain my hair appointments, I did cancel my nail appointments.

I cried and I saved and I made it through.

Now I am more aware of how I spend my money. I have decreased my spending on fast food, Starbucks, and clothing. I even occasionally place myself on mini-financial fasts!

Barbara

DAILY ASSIGNMENT

*What bonds have kept you from accepting God's abundance in your life?
Make a list of any financial bonds you can identify. For example, if you
know you are addicted to shopping, write about it in your journal. Why do
you think you have a problem with overspending? What might be missing
in your life that you try to make it up with shopping? You might explore
why you worry so much about money when you are financially secure.
Why can't you let go of the fear of being destitute? If you put people through
agony about the gifts they give or don't give, examine the motives behind
your ingratitude. Why do you think you might put so much emphasis on
what people give you? Why do you equate love to the material things you
receive?*

*After you've made your list, identify just one financial bond you will commit
to addressing. If it's something too deep to handle by yourself, get help. Seek
counseling.*

*If you are doing well financially, make a list of some things you've really
wanted and have the money for but haven't been able to bring yourself to
buy. Choose at least one thing from the list, and go buy it ... but not until
after the fast.*

Strengthen Stewardship

3 Days to Go: God's Trust Gained

Main Point: The better I handle the money I have, the more I may receive.

My Pledge: I will sign a quitclaim deed acknowledging that everything I have belongs to God.

You've probably heard the expression "be a good steward," but do you really know what it means? Merriam-Webster's defines a *steward* as "a fiscal agent" or one who "manages."

To be a *good steward* means you are managing well what God has given to you. It means understanding that all you have belongs to God. When God entrusts you with wealth, you become responsible for overseeing how it gets used.

You didn't get to where you are financially on your own. Consider these words from Deuteronomy: "You may say to yourself, 'My power and the strength of my hands have produced this wealth for me.' But remember the Lord your God, for it is he who gives you the ability to produce wealth, and so confirms his covenant, which he swore to your ancestors, as it is today" (Deut. 8:17 – 18). It wasn't your power that produced your prosperity. And if you're broke, it won't be by your own hands that you dig yourself out of debt. Show yourself to be a good steward, or that you are working on becoming a better money manager, and God will prosper you.

One way to remember that God owns everything is to turn everything over to him. You can do that today by signing a quitclaim deed. A quitclaim deed is a legal document in which you transfer the interest you may have in a property to someone else. For this exercise you will sign the deed over to God. He already owns everything, but this is a tangible acknowledgment of that fact.

The following is a copy of a quitclaim deed. You can find it at *www.michellesingletary.com*. Sign the deed and keep it in your journal.

Why bother with this? Because one day you are going to have to give an account of how you managed the resources entrusted to your care. How will you respond to this audit? Could you defend your actions and provide proof that you managed your time, talents, and

---

QUITCLAIM DEED

THIS QUITCLAIM DEED, Executed this _____ day of _____, 20____,

by said first party _____

certifies that all my real property and assets belong to God.

IN WITNESS WHEREOF, the said first party hereby acknowledges and does hereby release and quit claim unto God all the right, title, interest, and claims to said property.

Signed in the presence of:

_____   _____

     First Party (Your signature)   Witness (Your accountability partner)

> *Yours, Lord, is the greatness and the power*
>   *and the glory and the majesty and the splendor,*
>   *for everything in heaven and earth is yours.*
> *Yours, Lord, is the kingdom;*
>   *you are exalted as head over all.*
> (1 Chronicles 29:11)

treasures in a way that glorifies God? Or have you made a wreck of your finances, much like a careless family or friend may have damaged a car or squandered money they borrowed from you?

THE GOOD STEWARDS

This fast was designed in part to help those who have mismanaged money to become good stewards, and to strengthen the financial skills of those who are already managing well what they have. If you're already a good steward, think of the 21-day fast as a checkup, much like when you get the required maintenance on your car — which I hope you have been getting since it saves you money in the long run. If you haven't gotten regular maintenance on your car, the mechanic may chastise you for running your car into the ground. This would be similar to someone not taking good care of their finances. Or the mechanic may find nothing wrong with your car because you've taken good care of your vehicle. The mechanic may suggest some fine tuning to make sure your car continues to operate properly. That's the same as going through the fast even if your finances are good.

No matter where you were financially, participating in the fast should have helped you with everything from addressing serious problems to making the small adjustments that keep your finances running well. You might even consider doing the fast over and over again, perhaps once a year.

There is one thing I can say for sure about the many people who complete this fast. Those who stick with it do become better stewards over their money. Those who repeatedly do the fast continue to be challenged and learn something about themselves. They see their financial lives improve because they've shown they can be trusted with what they have. Mellissa has done the fast several times, and each time she says she makes adjustments to her finances in her quest to handle her money better.

The first time Mellissa did the fast, she cheated a bit.

"I honestly panicked and I immediately tried to come up with 'gimmicks of survival,'" she said. "I would double-pay my hairstylist and manicurist in advance so that technically I wasn't spending money that particular week of the fast."

The second time around, Mellissa did better.

"The second fast occurred during my birthday month, and I thought it would be hard," she said. "Ironically, I was unexpectedly dumped by my boyfriend, so dwelling on that overtook my desire to shop. I just wanted to stay home. That taught me that if you can place your mind on things that are more important, you really don't need to shop as a coping mechanism."

I love to hear the testimonies of people who are good stewards and who decide to do the fast. Repeatedly, they find some area where they can improve. Best of all, it strengthens their resolve to remain good stewards.

Juanita became a living testimony. She couldn't stop talking about how the fast changed her life.

"I really do thank God for the financial fast," she said. "I no longer have a desire to spend. I have truly replaced spending with saving. It is now painful for me to spend money, but painful in a positive way."

Trinita, Deenice, and Michael are examples of people who continue to complete the financial challenge even though they were good money managers to start. And yet even they say the fast highlighted areas for them where they could improve.

"The first time, for me, was the easiest," Trinita said. "It's more difficult now because circumstances have changed — I have a new home, a new hairstyle, and new eating habits." Trinita says the fast became harder because lack of money isn't an issue anymore. It's harder for her to stick to the fast because she can afford to spend. So during the fast it was easy to fall off the wagon. Even good money managers can stand to rein in their spending and credit card usage now and again.

Good stewardship is a lifelong job. As cheap as I am, I continue to find the fast challenging. I look at it as continuing education.

CHALLENGES CONQUERED

What I like best about this fast is the self-realizations people have about becoming better stewards. And for some that meant dealing with their "issues."

"The hardest thing was to admit that I had entitlement issues," Kiesha said, following her fast.

Barbara, a professional who was extremely competent on the job, finally admitted to herself that her personal finances were jacked up. The fast turned her around. She began saving, and when she got married, she had several thousand dollars to help out with the wedding. "I now keep my receipts to document my spending," Barbara said. "Can you imagine keeping a small pad with you at all times to record all of your spending habits? Well, I couldn't either, but I did it!"

One minister conquered her spendthrift ways, and now she mentors others who need to do the same. "The temptation comes and goes to spend on things that I don't need," Min. Michele said. "But at that moment, I begin to tell the Lord, 'Lord, I don't need that,' and the temptation goes away."

Is everyone a success story? No. However, far more people succeed than fail when they approach the fast by looking at it from a stewardship perspective. I know, for example, that if I borrow someone's car, I am careful to drive more safely or to park it in a good spot so it won't get dinged. The admonition of Scripture is to "guard what has been entrusted to your care" (1 Tim. 6:20). Remember, a good steward or manager will often be given more to take care of. But if you can't be trusted with what you have already, why should God give you more? Well, he probably won't.

TESTIMONY TIME: *Day 19*

We started following the financial freedom fast and began tracking our daily expenses. We had to laugh because our expense list the first month went a little like this:

- *Food, food, food*
- *Groceries, restaurant*
- *Tithes and offerings*
- *Restaurant*
- *Transportation, mortgage, and utilities*
- *Haircut, hairstyle*
- *Food, food, and more food*

We were so convicted after realizing that we buy groceries, eat at restaurants, and then throw leftover food away. We started splitting entrees when eating out to avoid leftovers, cooking more, and carrying lunch to work.

Jackie

DAILY ASSIGNMENT

If you are ready to acknowledge that God owns everything you have, go online, print out, and sign the quitclaim deed. If you honestly can't sign the deed, pray that God will help you realize he's in control.

Identify one area of your finances where you have been a good steward but where you may need some improvement. For example: "I use credit wisely, but I could stand to examine if I'm still spending more than I should."

Once you've identified one area of your finances that could be improved upon, determine what you can do to make it better. For example: Pull out your credit card statements for the last six months. Go over them and see if you can find a pattern of spending that you can reduce.

Relationships Rescued

2 Days to Go: Love Is Priceless

Main Point: Taking a break from consumption can help you focus on the most important relationships in your life.

My Pledge: I will call a close relative or friend with whom I have exchanged gifts in the past and come up with an agreement that on the next birthday, anniversary, or holiday, we will not spend money on each other but spend time with each other instead.

Take a moment. Breathe. You're almost done. It hasn't been so bad, right?

Okay, it may have been tough so far, but I've got to cheer you on to the finish line.

By now I hope you've learned a lot about both your finances and yourself. This journey hasn't been all about the money. Going through the fast and taking a break from consuming can help you focus and work on healing the most important relationships in your life.

One couple who participated in the fast was as close as you can get to filing for divorce. The only reason they hadn't filed, the wife said, was because they couldn't afford to hire attorneys. The tension in their relationship developed when the husband came close to losing his government job because his security clearance was pulled, because of the couple's bad credit. After budgeting, cutting their expenses, and participating in the fast, the husband's security clearance was reinstated. Most importantly, the drama in the couple's marriage abated. They attributed their rescued relationship in part to the fast.

TESTIMONY TIME: *Day 20*

I had a challenge during my fast. Even though my wife's birthday fell near the end of the fast, I did not wilt in the waning moments. I stayed strong, and despite the abuse I took for not doing what she said she wanted me to do, I created a birthday that she will remember forever. Instead of doing a big blowout for her birthday as I would normally do, I gathered all of her siblings and her parents and we cooked a meal. Then each person presented a memory about my wife from her childhood or her young adult life. This went off great and it didn't cost much. This fast is a good exercise that we will use from time to time to make sure that we are being good stewards of our finances.

Jaime

Shirley took the fast challenge during one February when she typically spent a lot on Valentine's Day presents and a card for her mother. It was a struggle for Shirley to curtail her spending. So when I challenged her to do the fast, I encouraged her to find another way to celebrate Valentine's Day. Shirley was reluctant at first — this was her mother, after all — but she finally yielded. Instead of an expensive gift, she wrote her mother a letter.

"I did not have a great relationship with my mother, and I had been asking God for a way to reach her and break the barrier that had separated us for so many years," Shirley said. "I've had a real hard life and wanted to discuss it with my mom, but she never wanted to talk about the past. With reluctance to share those intimate details, we just drifted apart.

"I received a phone call after she received the letter," Shirley continued. "My mother told me she didn't want to read it at first. She picked it up and put it down, picked it up and put it down again. She picked it up again and read 'Happy Valentine's Day.' But when she saw that it was seven pages long, she closed it again. It was just too long, my mother said. Then she got up enough nerve because she was really curious to find out why I had written her. Finally she opened it, began to read it, and did not put it down until she completed it. She said she laughed a little and cried a little, laughed a little, and cried a little. We've been talking almost every day since."

The healing Shirley found might have never happened had she continued to celebrate the holiday by buying something for her mother. So often we busy ourselves with shopping for our friends and family that we don't have the conversations we need to have. The presents become more important than our presence. We try to use the presents to express the love that only our words and actions can convey.

TESTIMONY TIME: *Day 20*

The fast has proven that we can work out our money issues and, at the same time, be freed up from burdens of financial hardship. We have paid off one credit card and a Thrift Savings Plan loan. We are not totally out of debt yet, but we are striving and making progress through God's Word.

Ronald and Mary

DAILY ASSIGNMENT

Think about all the relationships that are important to you. Have you spent more time shopping for these people than spending quality time with them? If you find that you have, call them up or write them a letter. Begin to bond with them without having to exchange a gift between you.

Don't forget your pledge. Call one close relative or friend and agree that on the next special occasion where a gift may be expected, you will not spend money on each other but instead spend time with each other.

Financial Freedom

Final Day: Financial Faithfulness

Main Point: If you really want to know what you value, look at where you spend your money.

My Pledge: I promise to find at least one other person to help go through the 21-day financial fast.

You made it to the last day! Praise God!

Go ahead and congratulate yourself. I'm certainly proud of you. Seriously, I am. I've done this fast several times, and despite my frugal ways, it's still tough. The fact that you chose to embark on this journey — even if you faltered along the way — is an indication of your commitment to a better financial life. It means you desire financial freedom. Doesn't it feel good to know that you can change or improve your finances for the better?

Over the last twenty-one days, we've covered a lot of territory. I've asked you to do several things, some that probably made you very uncomfortable. Rarely is anyone happy to do a budget. It's a pain and painful, especially if you realize you don't have enough income to cover your expenses. Yet budgeting is extremely vital to your financial life. If you skipped that exercise, I encourage you to go back to Day 7 and do it. As the Bible says, "The plans of the diligent lead to profit"

(Prov. 21:5). Don't be hardheaded. Don't make me have to call you a "sluggard" like in Proverbs 6:6. Instead, handle your finances like an ant who has "no commander, no overseer or ruler, yet it stores its provisions in summer and gathers its food at harvest" (Prov. 6:7–8).

You must budget. It's the foundation for financial freedom. You have to account for what's coming into your household and what's going out. Unless you complete at least that one task, you won't have anything to store up.

TESTIMONY TIME: *Day 21*

My greatest challenge was to keep the overall commitment. Just knowing nobody was watching me spend, my personal integrity was consistently being challenged, as it usually is living this Christian life.

I used Scripture to encourage me when I got weary. Scripture served as a steady diet of faith-building nuggets that encouraged me to see the fast through to the end.

Bethany

GOD'S BLUEPRINT FOR PROSPERITY

The point of this financial fast wasn't to set you up financially to acquire more things. It's to help enrich you so that you can bless others — in your family, in community, and in the world. That's the purpose of prosperity — to help others. I didn't make this up; it's right there in the Bible: "Command them to do good, to be rich in good deeds, and to be generous and willing to share" (1 Tim. 6:18).

What good is it for you to have money to buy a C-Class Mercedes Benz if you won't give someone else a ride? Or to selfishly take up two parking spaces because you don't want to get a ding in the door of your Benz! Why have a lavishly decorated home with multiple bedrooms and refuse to take in a relative or friend in need?

My husband and I have used our God-given prosperity to help

send a young woman, whom I met in a journalism class, to a community college. We have also assisted two nieces in paying their college expenses. When my brother and sister-in-law fell short of a down payment for their first home, we fronted them the money. At various times we've bailed out relatives. I'm telling you this not to brag but to encourage you to save up to help people beyond your nuclear family. Wouldn't you like to bless someone in your life?

Prosperity gives us the power to bless others, but it also poses temptations. There are plenty of warnings in the Bible about worshiping wealth. Perhaps one of the most well-known is this statement by Jesus: "Again I tell you, it is easier for a camel to go through the eye of a needle than for someone who is rich to enter the kingdom of God" (Matt. 19:24).

This warning, repeated again in Mark 10:25, is often misunderstood and interpreted as proof that God doesn't want you to prosper. But Christ wasn't condemning prosperity; he was making the point to his disciples that wealth can make it difficult to seek and receive salvation. Christ cautioned that we must learn to be content and avoid placing our faith in material things. It is the love of money, not money itself, that can stand in the way of our salvation.

God's plan for prosperity isn't a blueprint to become Rockefeller rich. However, I've discovered that if you follow God's Word, you can spend well and live rich — as long as you understand that living rich doesn't mean you're going to be blessed with a McMansion or a Mercedes. It may be that you are destined to live a modest life. It may be that you are destined to be six- or seven-figure wealthy. In either state, you need to learn to be content.

Can I be honest with you? I'm frequently asked to be on panels with successful entrepreneurs. Without fail, one of these business owners admonishes the audience for not striving to become their own boss. Mostly what they talk about is that you can get rich running your own business. Personally, I like working for a large corporation. My paycheck comes every two weeks. I have health insurance. I get paid vacation and sick leave. It's comfortable. I'm not sure I want to be responsible for other people's livelihoods. However, as it has turned out, in many ways I am an entrepreneur, but it's not something I chose because I was seeking wealth. I found this path following God's plan for my life.

There are many paths to prosperity. My grandmother, Big Mama, was rich by her standard with just $20,000 in a savings account when she retired. She lived a rich retirement because her wants were few. Living a rich life may mean following your dream to become a teacher or working in the public sector. It means not letting others discourage you from pursuing a certain career because there's little potential for a high-income salary.

I went to a seminar hosted by a prominent businessman who has sold millions of books pushing the shtick that everyone should be in real estate. During one of his presentations he criticized people who want to work a 9-to-5 job. You know what he called them? What he called me or perhaps you? A loser. He further illustrated his point by pressing his right index finger and thumb on his forehead in the shape of an "L." His advice was atrocious and insulting.

I believe we all have a God-given gift. And you can prosper in the pursuit of that gift. Not everyone should be in the real estate market. Not everyone should be an entrepreneur. The statistics on the failure rate of small businesses are proof of that. Some people should never be somebody's boss or be responsible for the livelihood of others. We all can't be doctors or lawyers or whatever occupation you think it takes to be rich.

Follow the principles presented in this book, and you can live well on a teacher's salary. Some of the people I admire the most, who have shaped and impacted my life the most, are educators. What a tragedy if they had abandoned their gift of teaching because they couldn't make a six-figure salary. If you're married and have children, these principles may allow you or your spouse to be a stay-at-home parent. On the other hand, if you want to own a business, that's fine too.

I pray that you will not limit your definition of what it means to be rich. It can mean having a lot of material things, but it also, and more importantly, means learning to live with less so that you can live your life more abundantly. It means having financial peace, which is priceless.

THIS IS JUST THE BEGINNING

The 21-day fast may be over, but your work isn't. If you're in debt, you didn't get into debt in such a short period of time, and you won't get out of debt in twenty-one days either. You've probably spent years mismanaging your money, so it's going to take time to break all those bad habits.

This fast is an outward sign that you are willing to change, and that's half the battle. So here's your next task: Over the next thirty days I want you to start keeping a spending journal, which is different from the daily journal you should have been using. In this journal I want you to track your daily expenditures.

For the next thirty days following the fast, you will record every penny you spend. In a notebook, on your computer, in your Blackberry, iPhone, or whatever method you prefer — record every penny, nickel, dime, quarter, and dollar you spend. This includes writing down monthly expenses such as your mortgage or rent, car payment, etc.

The fast temporarily put a stop to your spending and using credit; now I want you to track how you spend your money during a time of no restrictions. What you find may amaze you. Even those who were already good money managers and kept a spending journal have come to me later and said they never realized how much money they wasted.

After you've finished the fast, let me know how you did. I want to hear your testimonies. Email me at *colorofmoney@washpost.com*. In the subject line, put "21-Day Financial Fast." I also encourage you to share your stories with your family, friends, coworkers, and church members.

Although the fast is over, stay committed. And if you find your-self slipping, do the fast again. Will everything in your financial life improve in twenty-one days? No, probably not. But it's a start to examine what you value the most so that you can focus your money on those things. And while you may not be able to buy everything you want, you can live a prosperous life. The 21-day financial fast will put you on the path to financial peace and freedom.

DAILY ASSIGNMENT

On this final day of the fast, calculate how much you've saved by not spending during these last twenty-one days. You can do that by just looking at last month's credit card statement. Also look at your debit charges from the previous month.

Encourage at least one other person to go through the 21-day financial fast. Help someone else become a good steward. You can help change the legacy in your family or circle of friends by sharing what you have learned.

Starting tomorrow, begin keeping your 30-day spending journal. (See Appendix 2 on page 241.)

APPENDIXES

Blank Budget Worksheet

Note: Input your own figures into the blank fields. In the second column (% of Income for Major Categories), really examine the percentage you are spending in each major area, which is based on your Net Spendable Income.

INCOME	Pay Period 1	Pay Period 2	Pay Period 3	Pay Period 4	Pay Period 5	Monthly Totals
Wages/Salary/Tips	$	$				$
Commissions/Bonuses		$				$
Social Security/Pension/Retirement						$
Alimony						$
Child Support						$
Interest/Dividend Income						$
Disability, VA Benefits						$
Other Income						$
Total Gross Income	$	$	$	$	$	$
Net Income (Take-home pay)	$	$				$

Continued on next page

EXPENSES

	Pay Period 1	Pay Period 2	Pay Period 3	Pay Period 4	Pay Period 5	Monthly Totals
Total Gross Income	$	$	$	$	$	$
Net Income (Take-home pay)	$	$	$	$	$	$
Tithes (10% of Gross Income)	$	$	$	$	$	$
Net Spendable Income	$	$	$	$	$	$
Monthly Expenses	$	$	$	$	$	$
Difference	$	$	$	$	$	$

*The information for this top box (Net Spendable Income and Monthly Expenses) is pulled from the information you'll input for your monthly expenses. Negative numbers (in parentheses) mean you are spending more than your net spendable income. If so, then you need to reduce your expenses, increase your income, or both. On the other hand, if you have money left over after paying your expenses, use it to accelerate paying off debts and/or to increase your savings.

	Monthly Expenses Paid from Each Paycheck					Monthly Expense Total	Target Percentage	Actual Percentage
	Pay Period 1	Pay Period 2	Pay Period 3	Pay Period 4	Pay Period 5			
Savings	$	$	$	$	$	$	2-10%	7%
Emergency Savings						$		
Life Happens Savings Fund						$		
Retirement Savings						$		
College Savings						$		

Category								
Housing	$	$	$	$	$	$	26-36%	34%
Mortgage/Rent						$		
Home Equity Loan or Line of Credit (HELOC)						$		
Property Tax						$		
Home Owners'/Condo Association Dues/Fees						$		
Homeowner's/Renter's Insurance						$		
Utilities	$	$	$	$	$	$	4-8%	14%
Electricity						$		
Natural Gas/Oil						$		
Water/Sewer						$		
Phone (landline)						$		
Cell Phone						$		
Cable TV, Internet service						$		
Food	$	$	$	$	$	$	12-30%	17%
Groceries						$		
Meals Out						$		
Workplace lunch, snacks						$		
School lunch, snacks						$		

Continued on next page

237

Family Obligations	$	$	$	$	$	$	6-16%	0%
Child Support						$		
Alimony						$		
Childcare						$		
Private school tuition						$		
Music/Sports Lessons						$		
Nursing Home/Health Aid/Senior Care						$		
Transportation	$	$	$	$	$	$	6-15%	15%
Auto Payments						$		
Gasoline						$		
Auto Insurance						$		
Public transportation/parking						$		
Insurance (if not deducted from pay)	$	$	$	$	$	$	4%	0%
Medical						$		
Dental/Vision						$		
Life						$		
Disability						$		

Category								
Health Expenses	$	$	$	$	$	4%	0%
Medical/dental copays/Expenses	$						
Medications	$						
Medical Supplies	$						
Debt Payments	$	$	$	$	$	5-10%	10%
Credit Cards	$						
Student Loans	$						
Personal/401k Loans	$						
Giving	$	$	$	$	$	0%	0%
Charitable Giving (religious, private charity)	$						
Fees	$	$	$	$	$	0%	0%
Bank/Credit Union Account Fees	$						
Professional Services Fees	$						
Clothing	$	$	$	$	$	4-6%	0%
Clothing (family)	$						
Uniforms, accessories for work	$						

Continued on next page

							2-8%	3%
Entertainment/Recreation	$	$	$	$	$	$	$	
Entertainment/Activities	$					$		
Subscriptions/Dues						$		
Fitness /Spa						$		
Pets	$	$	$	$	$	$		0%
Food, grooming, etc.						$		
Veterinarian, pet insurance						$		
Miscellaneous	$	$	$	$	$	$		0%
Toiletries/Cosmetics/grooming						$		
Professional Membership Dues/Fees						$		
Other						$		
Investments	$	$	$	$	$	$		0%
Stocks, Bonds, CDs, Mutual Funds						$		
IRAs/Retirement						$		
Second Property Expenses						$		

What's Next: Starting Your 30-Day Spending Journal

Now that the fast is over, I want you to incorporate what you have learned into your daily life. And that can begin by tracking your spending.

Get a small notebook that you can easily carry with you. For the next thirty days, write down all the money you spend and what you spent it on. Include any bills you pay (mortgage, credit card, car loan). The point of this exercise is to record every single penny that you spend. Everything gets written down, even a pack of gum or bag of chips. Copy the following columns into your notebook, or you can make a photocopy of the chart below. Make sure to include the column identifying whether your purchase or payment was a need or a want. You can also download spending journal pages at *www.michellesingletary.com*.

Here's what your journal should include:

Day/Date	Expense Item	Amount Spent	Was this expense a need or a want?

Here's an example of what a journal entry may look like on a particular day:

Day/Date	Expense Item	Amount Spent	Was this expense a need or a want?
Mon./Sept. 10	Sausage, Egg McMuffin Meal @ McDonald's	$5.67	It was a want because I could have eaten breakfast before I left for work.
Mon./Sept. 10	Starbucks Grande Latte	$3.95	Want
Mon./Sept. 10	Lunch at Subway (turkey sandwich, drink, chips)	$6.97	Need, maybe. I didn't pack a lunch??
Mon./Sept. 10	Snack bag of UTZ from vending machine	.75	Need/want. I don't know. I was hungry!!!
Mon./Sept. 10	Late fee (was 5 minutes late picking up my son)	$10	Not sure. I needed to pay the fee to get my kid.
Mon./Sept. 10	Dinner from Popeye's	$24.35	Okay, a want. But I was too tired to cook.

KEEPING TRACK

You won't start the spending journal until after you have completed the 21-day fast.

Use the spending journal to record what you spend. Don't edit or judge yourself. This exercise works best if, for the thirty days, you simply record what you do.

After thirty days, go back and look at your spending patterns and habits. Make a note of where and when you tend to get off track concerning budgeted expenses.

Use the information from your spending journal to make adjustments to your budget (which you should have in place by now, right?). For example, if you are routinely late picking up your child from school and incur additional charges for child care, you need to build that expense into your budget. Otherwise leave work earlier, or work out an arrangement with another parent to help you pick up your child on time so you can avoid late fees.

How to Start a 21-Day Fast in Your Church

All Scripture is God-breathed and is useful for teaching, rebuking, correcting and training in righteousness, so that the servant of God may be thoroughly equipped for every good work.

2 Timothy 3:16 – 17

You could do a great service in your community if you encouraged your church family to undertake a 21-day financial fast. You could help your church members get their finances straight by organizing fasting groups.

If you are a minister or pastor, you could designate a twenty-one-day period and encourage your congregation to complete the fast together. This is a great way to help your members become better stewards. In fact, this would be a wonderful activity to hold before a stewardship campaign. It will prepare your members to give as well as help them find the money to give.

Another way to start a fast in your church is to work through individual ministries. Your choirs, singles, Bible study, Sunday school, or drama ministries could each conduct a fast. The great thing about this approach is that members have a built-in support network. During regular meetings while the fast is going on, each ministry can set aside time to talk about the fast, sharing stories, tips, or frustrations. They can make it a group project. This would be a perfect exercise if you have a financial ministry or classes in your Bible institute.

I'm sure your members have a lot of financial issues this fast could help address. It can help you develop dynamic disciples, spreading the word of good stewardship by example.

Sample Daily Fast Journal Page

See the sample journal page below for an illustration that will give you an idea of what to write in your fast journal. Don't edit yourself—just put to paper your feelings. In your journal, write about the daily assignments that I ask you to complete.

This is your private talk with yourself and God. You don't have to share it with anyone. Or if you want, share your personal observations with your fast accountability partner. The main thing is to journal, which shows discipline.

Today's date: *January 1, 2014*   *Day 1 of the Fast*

What I am feeling today about my finances:

For years I've been concerned about my money. I pay bills late. I never have money for emergencies, such as when my car needed repairs recently. I would rob Peter to pay Paul, but now they're both broke. I screen my calls because I can't stand getting all those calls from creditors. I'm at a loss as to how to change my bad money habits. HELP!

What was easy about the fast today:

Day 1 and I made it through without spending any money. It was actually not so hard because I took my lunch to work and also my snacks. For the first time in a long time, I had a $20 bill at the beginning of the day, and at the end of the day I still had the same $20. It's a miracle!

What was hard about the fast today:

The hardest part of the fast was not eating lunch out with my coworkers. They all came around like they normally do. I watched as they all were laughing and talking on their way out of the building. And there I was, sitting at my desk with my brown paper bag lunch. I worried I would be missing out on the goings-on in the office. Will they be talking about me? What will they think if I don't eat lunch with them for the next three weeks?

What I learned from today's chapter:

Dear God, I can do this. I'm so sick and tired of being broke. I want so desperately to stop worrying about money. But I learned I do have the discipline to stop spending. I just have to plan.

I am going to apply what I learned in the following ways:

1. I'm going to make an effort to get up early and make my lunch.
2. I'm going to start thinking about why I spend so much. I grew up poor, so maybe that's why I can't deny myself things I know I can't afford. It's funny, I never really thought about how deprived I felt as a child.

Financial Fast Scripture Verses

Throughout the Bible there are hundreds of Scriptures to help guide you on your journey to financial freedom. Below you will find some of my favorites. I've organized them in a way to give you scriptural grounding for each concept, starting with tithing:

TITHE AND OFFERINGS

"Bring all the tithes into the storehouse,
That there may be food in My house,
And try Me now in this,"
Says the LORD of hosts,
"If I will not open for you the windows of heaven
And pour out for you such blessing
That there will not be room enough to receive it."

MALACHI 3:10 NKJV

Honor the Lord with your possessions,
And with the firstfruits of all your increase;
So your barns will be filled with plenty,
And your vats will overflow with new wine.

PROVERBS 3:9 – 10 NKJV

GIVING

Give, and it will be given to you. A good measure, pressed down, shaken together and running over, will be poured into your lap. For with the measure you use, it will be measured to you.

LUKE 6:38

BUDGETING

Suppose one of you wants to build a tower. Won't you first sit down and estimate the cost to see if you have enough money to complete it?

LUKE 14:28

Whoever disregards discipline comes to poverty and shame, but whoever heeds correction is honored.

PROVERBS 13:18

EMERGENCY FUND

Go to the ant, you sluggard;
    consider its ways and be wise!
It has no commander,
    no overseer or ruler,
yet it stores its provisions in summer,
    and gathers its food at harvest.

PROVERBS 6:6 – 8

"LIFE HAPPENS" FUND

The wise store up choice food and olive oil,
but fools gulp theirs down.

PROVERBS 21:20

RETIREMENT SAVINGS

Through wisdom a house is built,
And by understanding it is established.

PROVERBS 24:3 NKJV

COLLEGE FUND

Anyone who does not provide for their relatives, and especially for their own household, has denied the faith and is worse than an unbeliever.

1 Timothy 5:8

A good person leaves an inheritance for their children's children, but a sinner's wealth is stored up for the righteous.

Proverbs 13:22

EXTRA CASH TO PAY DOWN DEBTS

Do not withhold good from those to whom it is due,
When it is in the power of your hand to do so.
Do not say to your neighbor,
"Go, and come back,
And tomorrow I will give it,"
When you have it with you.

Proverbs 3:27 – 28 NKJV

Index

A

AARP, 201
aarp.org/home-family/caregiving
.com, 197
adult children, 43, 55 – 56
adultery, 44
advance directives, 299
advertising, 80, 84 – 85
affinity fraud, 191
aging, 194 – 202
ambition, selfish, 129
arrogance, 129
asset allocation, 121 – 25
assisted-living facilities, 197
ATMs, 122 – 23
attitude of gratitude, 79 – 81

B

bank accounts, 129
banking, online, 172
bankrate.com, 111, 112
bankruptcy, 64, 160 – 61
Bible, 17, 150 – 51
birthday parties, 29 – 30
blessings, 79
bondage, financial, 25 – 38,
    213 – 17
bonds, 122
Boomerang Generation, 43 – 44
borrowing, 113, 125, 151.
    See also loans
    guidelines for, 153 – 54
budgets/budgeting, 88 – 106,
    228
    basics of, 98 – 99
    benefits of, 89 – 91
    building, 91 – 92

guidelines for a strong start,
    95 – 98
sample worksheet, 100 – 105
Scripture, 247
suggested percentages for major
    items, 99
and teens, 143, 146
template for, 92 – 95
worksheet, 235 – 40
businesses in a box, 191
business.gov/guides/franchises, 191

C

caregivers, 194 – 202
caremanager.org, 201
cars, purchasing, 112 – 13
car-title loans, 42
cash, 122 – 23
cash reserves, 124
cell phones, 45, 78
certificates of deposit (CDs), 112
cheapness, 53
children
    adult, 43, 55 – 56
    and credit, 172 – 73
    and money, 134 – 46
    needs of, 136 – 37
college, saving for, 119, 139 – 42,
    144, 157, 248
Colossians 3:18, 66
commandments. See Ten
    Commandments
compassion, 49
complaining, 85
conceit, vain, 129
Consumer Financial Protection
    Bureau, 140, 141

consumerism, 18
contentment, 80, 82–87
cosigning, 177–85
coveting, 44–45, 85, 150
credit, 108, 166–76
    and children, 172–73
    true cost of, 174–75
Credit Card Accountability
    Responsibility and Disclo-
    sure Act, 171
credit cards, 18, 30–32, 168
    and authorized users, 182–84
    how to handle debt wisely,
        171–72
    and spending habits, 31,
        169–71
    and teens, 138
creditors, 158–59, 160, 161
credit unions, 123

D
Daniel 10:3, 28
Davies, Greg, 31
debit cards, 18–19, 30–33
debtadvice.org, 160, 164
Debt Dash Plan (DDP),
    161–64
debts, 115, 125, 149–65, 248.
        See also borrowing; specific
        type of loan
    consumer, 157
    and cosigning, 180–81
    credit card, 168, 171–72
    and entitlement, 75
    good, 152–53
    honoring, 64
    ignoring, 157–60
    reduction plans, 161–62
    and teens, 143
    and tithing, 64
    what Bible says about, 150–51

deceit, 54
deductions, tax, 156
Department of Veteran Affairs,
    U.S., 200
desires. *See* wants
Deuteronomy 8:17–18, 218
disability insurance, 124
discipline, 17, 108
discontentment, 86
dishonesty, 54
diversification, 119–25
divorce, 44, 128
Dunn, Lucia, 173

E
earning power, 130
Ecclesiastes
    2:10, 75
    2:11, 75
    5:5, 158
    7:14, 215
    10:19, 41
    11:2, 120
eldercare.gov, 201
elderly, 194–202
Elisha, 51–52, 154
emergency fund, 110–13, 115, 123,
        143, 157, 247
end-of-life wishes, 200
entertainment, 80, 138
entitlement, 73–81
entrepreneurship, 230
Ephesians
    5:22–24, 66
    5:33, 66
equilibrium, state of, 86
equities, 121
Exodus
    20:8, 43
    20:12, 43
    20:14, 44

20:15, 44
20:17, 44
expenditures, daily, 231
expenses, medical, 160

F

Fair Credit Billing Act, 168
Fair Debt Collection Practices
    Act, 158–59
famine, 108–9
fasting, 17. *See also* financial fast
fear, 213–14
Federal Deposit Insurance
    Corporation, 122
Federal Trade Commission,
    184–85
fees, 95–96
    credit cards, 171
    mutual funds, 121
    overdraft, 19, 32
    prepayment, 157
financial fast
    Scripture verses, 246–48
    starting one with church
        members, 243
    tips for, 36–37
    what can and can't be pur-
        chased during, 33–35
    what it is, 28–30
    why do it, 23
Financial Industry Regulatory
    Authority (FINRA), 123
financial planning, long-term,
    88
1 Chronicles 29:11, 219
1 Corinthians 3:19, 17
1 John 4:18, 132
1 Timothy
    5:8, 248
    6:9, 190
    6:17, 175

6:18, 228
6:20, 222
529 college savings plans,
    142–43
fixed income bonds, 122
401(k) retirement plans, 120, 142
fraud, 149–50, 189–90, 191, 202
freedom, financial, 151, 227–32
frugality, 53–54, 114–16
ftc.gov, 192

G

generosity
    generational, 55–57
    God's, 48–57
Genesis
    2:24, 128
    41:47–49, 108
    41:56–57, 109
    42:1–2, 109
    45:4–5, 109
get-rich quick schemes, 188,
    189–90, 190–92
gifts, God-given, 230
giving, 246
God
    generosity of, 48–57
    and money, 35, 41–42
    promise of prosperity, 45
gold, 125
grace, 49
gratitude, 79–81
greed, 150, 186–93
gross income, 62–63

H

Henry, Matthew, 178
hoarding, 53
Holy Spirit, 35, 67
"House Rules," 130–32
housing, 98, 114, 120, 150

252   21-DAY FINANCIAL FAST

I

illness, 194 – 202
income
  fixed, 124
  gross *vs.* net, 62 – 63
  and spending, 98
  and tithing, 63
inflation, 119, 120, 121
inheritance, 66, 144
in-home care, 197
insufficient-funds charges, 32
insurance, 124, 200
  life, 66
  long-term care, 197 – 99
insureuonline.org, 124
interest, 156, 171
investments/investing, 119 – 25
  borrowing for, 125
  guidelines for, 123
  inappropriate, 189 – 90
  minimizing losses, 120
  scams, 191
  tax-deferred, 142
  when young vs when older, 122,
    123
investopedia.com, 125
Investor Protection Trust, 202

J

James 4:1 – 2, 192
Jeremiah 22:21, 109
Jesus
  and tithing, 60 – 62
  ultimate sacrifice of, 52
Job 22:21, 211
John
  10:10, 41
  14:27, 207
joint bank accounts, 127 – 29
Joseph, 108 – 9

journaling, 20, 231, 241 – 42,
    244 – 45

L

Leviticus 27:30, 64
"life happens" fund, 110 – 13, 123,
    143, 157, 247
life insurance, 66, 124
living will, 200
living within one's means, 138,
    139, 143
loans. *See also* borrowing
  car-title, 42
  payday, 41 – 42
  student, 139 – 41, 152
long-term care, 194 – 202
Luke
  6:38, 61, 246
  6:40, 137
  7:41 – 42, 161
  8:14, 216
  12:16 – 21, 186
  12:22 – 30, 189
  12:48, 52
  14:28, 247

M

Malachi
  3:8, 65
  3:10, 61, 66, 68, 246
Mark 10:25, 229
marriage
  and money, 127 – 33
  and secrets, 131
  standard policies in, 131 – 32
  and tithing, 65 – 66
Matthew
  5:17, 60
  6:24, 151
  6:33, 41

19:24, 229
23:23, 61
Medicaid, 198
medical expenses, 160
medical power of attorney, 200
Medicare, 197 – 98
MedlinePlus.com, 200
mental recession, 115 – 16
michellesingletary.com, 20, 91,
    219, 241
miserliness, 52 – 55
money
    as cause of stress, 209 – 10
    managing, 134
    and marriage, 127 – 33
    spending, 215
    teaching children about,
        134 – 46
    and teenagers/young adults,
        137 – 38
    tips for saving, 97
money-market deposit account,
    112
money-market mutual funds, 122,
    123
MoreBusiness.com, 80
mortgages, 150, 152, 154 – 57
Moses, 61
multi-level marketing schemes,
    191
mutual funds, 121, 122, 123
myfdicinsurance.com, 122

N
naic.org, 198
nasaa.org, 191
National Association of Consumer
    Bankruptcy Attorneys, 140
National Association of Insurance
    Commissioners, 124, 198
National Association of Profes-
    sional Geriatric Care
    Managers, 201
National Institutes of Health, 200
needs, 45, 77, 86
net income, 62 – 63, 98
net worth, 114, 117 – 18
North American Securities
    Administrators Association,
    191
nursing homes, 197

O
obedience, 17
offerings, 65, 246
overdraft fees, 19, 32
overspending, 87, 140 – 41

P
parents, aging, 199 – 202
parties, birthday, 29 – 30
payday lenders, 41 – 42
P-A-Y regimen, 37
peace, financial, 207 – 12
peer pressure, 140
pensions, 67
Philippians
    2:3 – 4, 129
    4:12, 85
    4:19, 45
piggybacking, 182 – 84
planning, financial, 88
plenty, 86
Ponzi schemes, 191
poverty, 213
power of attorney, 200
Prelec, Drazen, 170
prepayment penalties, 157
pride, 77, 129
priorities, financial, 80

prosperity. *See also* wealth
    embracing, 213–17
    God's blueprint for, 228–31
    parents', 55–57
    promise of, 39–47
    on purpose, 14–21
    responsibilities of, 50–52
    sharing, 49
Prosperity Partners Ministry, 28,
    40
Proverbs
    1:5, 130
    3:9–10, 246
    3:27–28, 248
    6:1–5, 178–79
    6:5, 182
    6:6, 228
    6:6–8, 247
    6:7–8, 228
    11:15, 178
    13:7, 214
    13:11, 190
    13:18, 247
    13:22, 248
    15:27, 150
    17:18, 178
    21:5, 228
    21:20, 247
    22:6, 172
    22:7, 151
    22:26–27, 178
    24:3, 247
    27:1, 151
    27:13, 178
Psalms
    25:9, 37
    37:7, 192
    37:21, 158
    37:21a, 64
    37:23, 89

Q
quitclaim deed, 219

R
rate of return, 121
recession
    of 2007, 108, 120, 124
    mental, 115–16
    and scams, 189
relationships, 224–26
resources, God's, 52, 88
retirement, 119, 123–24
    and mortgage debt, 155
    saving for, 157, 247
riches, sharing, 52
risk, 120, 123, 124
Romans 12:2, 153

S
Sabbath, 43
saving, 107–18
    for college, 119, 139–42,
        142–43, 144, 157, 248
    for retirement, 157, 247
    and teens, 143
    tips for, 97
savings accounts, 110–13
scams, 149–50, 189–90
sec.gov/investor/pubs, 124
2 Chronicles 31:12, 65
2 Corinthians
    8:9, 52
    9:6–7, 62
    9:6–8, 65
2 Kings
    4:3–4, 154
    4:6, 154
    4:7, 154
    4:8–37, 51
2 Timothy 3:16–17, 243

secrets, 131
Securities and Exchange Com-
    mission, 125
self-absorption, 49
self-centeredness, 49
self-control, 78, 80
self-importance, 129
selfish ambition, 129
self-righteousness, 49
self-storage industry, 188
self-worth, 130
shopping, 18, 29, 80, 138
Shunammite woman, 51
Simester, Duncan, 170
Small Business Association, 191
Social Security, 67, 124
spending, 27
    comparing with net income, 98
    and housing, 98
    when using credit cards,
        31 – 32, 169 – 71
spending journal, 231, 241 – 42
spendthrifts, 55
splurges, 214 – 15
stealing, 44, 54
stewardship, 88, 218 – 23
stocks/stock market, 120, 121
stress, 209 – 10
student loans, 139 – 41, 152
surety, 177

T
take-home pay, 98
teenagers
    and budgets, 146
    and credit, 172 – 73
    and money, 137 – 38

temptation, 29, 75, 78, 87, 229
Ten Commandments, 42 – 45,
    46 – 47
"Time is Money" calculator, 80
tithing, 58 – 69, 143, 246
    and debt, 64
    and Jesus, 60 – 62
    and marriage, 65 – 66
    ten questions about, 62 – 67
Tufano, Peter, 170

U
unemployment, 63

V
vain conceit, 129
veterans, 200

W
wants, 45, 76, 77, 85
wealth. *See also* prosperity
    and the Bible, 17
    sharing, 52
    worshiping, 229
Womack, Greg, 123
work-at-home scams, 191
worry, 189

ZONDERVAN®